Fragments of Life

Fragments of Life

Al Staggs

THE INTERMUNDIA PRESS

THE INTERMUNDIA PRESS, LLC
Warrenton, Virginia

Fragments of Life
© 2013 by Al Staggs. All rights reserved.
Published 2013.
Printed in the United States of America.
ISBN 978-1-887730-29-7

No part of this book may be reproduced or transmitted in any form or by any means, electronic or mechanical, including photocopying, recording, or by information storage and retrieval system, without written permission from the publisher.

To order additional copies of this book, contact:

THE INTERMUNDIA PRESS

www.intermundiapress.weebly.com

*Dedicated to my wife Carol,
my soul mate,
who has lovingly and painstakingly
edited this volume.*

Contents

Preface	ix
Sacred Spaces	1
Retrospectives	23
Lights for the Journey	57
Perspectives	87
Vicissitudes	135
Posterity	169
Extravagant Gestures	189
Coming Home	213
Prayers	227
Time and Age	239

Preface

THIS COLLECTION OF POETRY is a journal representing observations, thoughts, and emotions that I have penned over a forty-year span. Some of my perspectives have evolved over the years; others have remained static. The constant thread is my lifelong preoccupation with the concept of time.

Although many of these selections were prompted by specific circumstances or occurrences, I think of this volume in its entirety as a composite of the human experience—an emotional road map that incorporates the expressions of gratefulness, sorrow, joy, anxiety, fear, spirituality, depression and hope that are common to all of us.

Sacred Spaces

Many people die with their music still in them. Why is this so? Too often it is because they are always getting ready to live. Before they know it, time runs out.

— Oliver Wendell Holmes

Retreat

Across the lake
and over the hill,
in the next county,
tall aspens shimmer
in the sunlight.

It's a place of retreat,
renewal, restoration
for the weary spirit.
Wooded walkways
become sanctuaries
from the clamorous
world of our work.

Time stops here,
the past catches us
and the future
is given new clarity.

Fragments of Life

Moonlit Night

It is another one
of those moonlit
starry nights.
A soft cool breeze,
the aroma of pine trees
and honeysuckle,
and my senses
take the cue.

I sit here staring
at the heavens
remembering
moonlit nights
at sixteen or so
when I responded in
much the same way.
It's good to still
feel this way after
all these years.

Sacred Spaces

Old Pine Tree

Tall old pine of the great forest,
I played beneath your branches
as a small boy,
yelling and laughing.

I swung from your branches
in my teens,
screaming like Tarzan
as I dropped from limb to limb
wearing nothing but a loin cloth.

As a young man of twenty-one
I spoke romantic words of love
to a beautiful young lass
beneath your silent branches.

Years and years of picnics
with children and grandchildren
were spent here
in your presence, old tree.
There was always music
and discussion of whatever issues
we thought were urgent then.

Fragments of Life

I am here again,
now well beyond eighty,
alone with just the sound
of the breeze rustling through
your mighty branches.
How I love you, old tree,
and how I resent you.
I love you for your presence
in those special moments
and I resent you
because you will live on
while we mortals,
after our short time here,
return to dust.

Sacred Spaces

Big Old House

It was our house,
grand, historic,
with memories
of only two
prior families.

It was our home,
a place made homey
with the passage
of time and life.

It was our house,
a perfect place
for an idyllic life.

It was our house,
a place with rooms
for social gatherings
and rooms for solitude.

That grand, historic
house was our house,
but only for a while.

Tree Outside the Window

It's the middle of October,
1996, in South Carolina.
I put my luggage down
on the floor of my motel room
and look out the window.

My eyes are treated
to the brilliant foliage
of a grand old oak tree
just outside the room.
I am mesmerized by the fact
that this new motel is located
in a setting that only nature
could have created.
Humankind has encroached
upon a sacred space
that was an ancient forest.

Motionless, I gaze for minutes
and consider the exposed roots
of the magnificent tree that strives
to stake its permanence
in the face of the undaunted,
ever-impinging march of progress
just beyond its roots.

Sacred Spaces

During this tiring journey
I shall gratefully rest
my body and spirit tonight,
and I will find comfort
in the long-standing shadow
of an old oak tree.

Sunset

Don't let the night
come down and take away
this lovely sunset.
The stunning red sky most certainly
redeemed this woeful day.
I am appalled that
dark thoughts in my mind
can sometimes cause me
to forget the gifts of creation.

It's something wonderful
how a sunset can transpose
the minor key of our trivial trials
into a rapturous major key,
a symphony of nature's beauty.

Lovely sunset, lovely sunset,
stay where you are,
stay where you are.

Spaces

Empty spaces are needed
in the pockets and places of our lives.
Unnecessary things take up
far too much room
in those silent, holy areas.

Our busy minds need
the time and the room
to expand, to roam within,
to transcend the ordinary.
The only furnishings required
are a chair, a desk
and a window to the sky

As years elapse,
the collection of things
has less appeal
and collecting memories
becomes more of a necessity.

My spirit's house will one day
wave farewell to the tangible,
to the world of things,
and will go in search of places
that are not bound by walls
of space and time.

Fragments of Life

Santa Fe

Indefinable,
deeply spiritual—
the mountains, the air,
the sense that this
is sacred space.
A place of sanctuary
in the midst of modernity
where generations
of Native people have lived
and passed on to spirit.

Yet their spirits remain here
and we are here
sharing the land they cherished.
This ancient city
reminds us of our transience
and our permanence.

Although the day will come
when my body no longer
walks this sacred earth,
my spirit,
the part of me that responds
to these surroundings,
will remain
here in Santa Fe
for we are connected
eternally.

Sacred Spaces

Quiet Place

How I long for a serene, quiet place
where sounds are soft and low,
a place that shows me nature's face,
where hurry cannot go.

Give me a restful, quiet place
where dreams of bliss and peace
give hope and sight to our frantic race,
to our souls a sweet release.

Out Under the Stars

Out under the stars
where the desert wind blows
let's hide from our sorrow,
let's hide from all our woes.

Join me in a gentle journey
free from pressure and pain.
Go to the desert with me
and let's begin life again.

Out under the glowing moon
your feelings will come alive.
Put your hand in mine,
our romance we will revive.

The desert sands call to you,
a dream world awaits you there.
Come on out and join me,
there's love and music in the air.

October Again

It's October again.
New Mexico—
the stately mountains,
the luminous moon
and sparkling stars.
New-fallen leaves
cover the earth.
The evergreens
and aspens dot
the morning sky
with brilliant color.

My eyes are playing
a concerto to my soul.
Nature meets nature—
a love relationship
from something intangible
within me falling in love
with the ambience of fall.

It is sensual, spiritual,
emotional, mystical,
outside the cognitive.
Let me bask in the sight,
the heady fragrance,
the cool chill of October
in the mountains.

Fragments of Life

Moon Watch
AUGUST 31, 1996

The moon surprised me tonight,
taking me back to
other memorable moon sightings
of the past.

September, 1980:
the weather was just turning
from unbearable summer heat
to the coolness of a fall breeze.
An Arkansas autumn
suddenly became romantic, other-worldly
through the presence of that heavenly body.

September, 1982:
Glorieta, New Mexico,
so enchanting,
like the state,
was the moon that night.
Cool breezes,
the scent of pinon
and the skies so clear
as only New Mexico can afford.
The stark, stunning sight of the moon
whose seductive light appeals to
my deepest longings
for connection to nature.

Sacred Spaces

All life is here, now.
All history has brought this moment
and this moment gives purpose to future.
Moon over my head,
moon in my heart.

Meet Me There

When stress, worry and struggle
diminish the light of life,
take a little time off
and meet me there.

Meet me where the lights are dim,
where voices are soft and low,
where everyone is a friend.

Meet me where folks
laugh, sing and dance,
where love and joy rule the day,
where peace and rest rule the night.

When the grind of daily drudgery
takes its toll on your aching heart,
run away from all that
and get a brand new start.

Meet me there,
there on the seashore
where the water is warm
and the beach is bare.
Come play in the sand with me.
Meet me there,
meet me there.

Sacred Spaces

Looking Up

O Moon,
you are so grand,
so removed.
O Sky,
you are so vast
and so beautifully adorned
by the floating clouds.

Tonight I look to you
to help me escape the trap
of my narrowness.
If I can just take my eyes
off the ground
and forget all that hems me in,
my spirit can soar to you,
O Moon,
and to you,
O Sky.

Ideal Place

Transplanting myself
to the mountaintop,
gazing at the glittering aspens,
mesmerized by deep blue skies
on which are etched
the tops of evergreens.

It's 9,000 feet above sea level,
above the sea of stress,
anxiety and mundane demands.

Time stands still here
at the top of the world.
This is a place like no other.
The eyes, mind and heart are at rest,
renewing their love for creation.

Sacred Spaces

Glorieta Garden

The wind whispers to me
through the aspen and fir
about other days and times
when I stood in this garden,
those times when concerns of life,
of marriage, of children
weighed heavily upon me,
times when I sought direction
for the right path to follow.

Now I am far, far down
the path of life.
Years have passed
and so much has changed.
Yet I remember still the prayers
I voiced on numerous occasions
as I wandered through
this serene and tranquil garden.
To visit here is to revisit
the memories of my heart.

Retrospectives

And in the end, it's not the years in your life that count. It's the life in your years.

— Abraham Lincoln

Past as Present

It is a myth to assume
that what is past is completed
and thus no longer worthy of reflection,
for the past remains in our memories.
Previous events continue to affect
our thought processes in the
course of our lives long after
the original episodes.

The old experiences
are replayed again and again
and given added significance
with the passing of time.
To understand our insecurities,
phobias, addictions and aversions
we must grapple
with the ghosts of the past.

Vulnerable are we when young.
Impressions and fears
are embedded deep within,
so deep that we live our past
as we live our present and future.

Days go by, years slip away,
but our todays and tomorrows
only confirm and expand the reality
that the echoes of our childhood
endure until we lie down
for our final sleep.

Fragments of Life

Barracks of Fort Polk

In the fall of September, 1965,
I was plucked from the security of my home
and assigned to live in close quarters
with African-Americans, Latinos, Texans,
Yankees, rednecks and other guys who hailed
from places far from where I'd been raised.
We were all strangers to one another
with widely-varying accents.
By the second week I began to wonder
if there was anything that
could bond together such a diverse group
whose cultural differences appeared
to prohibit finding any common ground.

Long days and rigorous training
coupled with strict and harsh discipline
that was equally applied by African-American,
Latino and Caucasian drill sergeants
ultimately molded us into a family
bound by a sense of duty that transcended
all of the things that originally divided us.

Retrospectives

On the day of graduation
we marched past the reviewing stand
in lock-step precision as One.
We had discovered that our diversity
had become one of our strengths
in spite of the fears we harbored
at the beginning of our eight arduous weeks
living in the barracks of Fort Polk.

Fragments of Life

When We Were Soldiers

In 1965 most of us draftees were still teenagers
training to kill Charlie, the Viet Cong, any way we could—
with rifle, machine gun, rocket launcher, grenade,
bayonet or by hand to hand combat.
My mind kept spinning with the incongruity
between that training and the thought
that just a few weeks before I had been sitting
in a pew at the Highway Baptist Church,
a rural church in Arkansas where my faith in God began,
the place where my convictions
concerning right and wrong had been nurtured.

In the wretched heat of Fort Polk, Louisiana,
I carried an M-16 rifle over my shoulder,
preparing to wage war on a people I didn't know.
Sgt. Campbell, a tough but fair African American drill sergeant,
reminded us often during those sweltering days of
gut-wrenching training that we became MEN
when we put on our army greens.
All of us had given our oaths to lay down our lives
in the defense of our nation, and Sgt. Campbell
convinced us that our lives depended on
our being physically and emotionally ready
to take out Charlie before Charlie could take us out.

Retrospectives

I was fortunate to be spared the experience
of serving in Vietnam during my two-year hitch.
Thousands of others were not so fortunate.
Many came home in body bags.
Many came home crippled and scarred.
Many more returned with no visible scars
but with invisible wounds that would never heal.
What those men experienced was hell on earth.

Our generation of soldiers came home
to a nation that was divided over the issue
of the American engagement in Vietnam.
There were no parades for returning Nam vets.
My comrades were not treated as heroes
like the soldiers who returned from World War II.
I have often thought of those days and
those brave men, some of whom were every bit as
courageous as Audie Murphy or Alvin York.

I think of them now when I travel through airports
and look into the eyes of the new generation of men
and women who proudly wear their uniforms.
I never fail to extend my hand to thank them
for their commitment and their service.

Yet, as I remember the painful lessons of Vietnam
and consider the present conflicts that are
stealing the lives, the well-being, the innocence
of brave young people, I wonder if this nation
will ever learn any lessons from its past.
Even McNamara apologized for Vietnam
but no one is apologizing for Afghanistan and Iraq.
We are mired in our own blood and the blood
of tens of thousands of innocent civilians.

To set the record straight, it is not our soldiers
who are ultimately to blame for the carnage of our wars.
The responsibility for this savagery is squarely on the
shoulders of the elected officials who make
the decisions in the halls of government,
far removed from the horror of the wars they initiate.
And the apathy of the American people
must bear a portion of the responsibility as well.

So now, in this stage of my life, the commitment
I made to God before my training for war
means working diligently for peace and justice
in this nation and throughout the world.
I was a soldier and am a soldier still.
At this point, though, every muscle and every fiber
of my being is aimed at a higher service.
I was a soldier and a soldier I will remain.

Those Were the Days

Those were the days.
We lived out our scripts with only
partial understanding of what we were doing
as life was being presented to us.

Now, many years later, we look back
and reflect upon all that has happened.
And as we remember, it seems
both so clear and yet so mysterious
how we arrived at this moment
in our journeys.

Those were the days when
we were growing in our understanding
of ourselves and the complexities
we were facing with each new sunrise.

Now, these are the days.
We continue to build on the former times.
We write our life stories as we are living them.
We are consigned to live with manifold regrets
accompanied by cherished memories.
We cannot change the past.
We can only hope to use it for our betterment.

Fragments of Life

While yesterday is past, it laid the foundation
for what we have come to be.
We hope and yearn to do better,
to be better so the memories and recollections
of those who follow us will be
treasured in their hearts and minds.

Those were the days.
And these are the days.

Retrospectives

PROM NIGHT

All decked out, dressed to the nines,
I nervously walked onto the dance floor
to celebrate the music of our time
and the time of our lives
with my classmates of the Class of '64.
For one evening, nothing else mattered.
Not grades, not world events, not future plans.
Past and future were welded together
on that magical night with its aromas
of English Leather and Ambush.

We laughed and danced
and forgot about the world around us.
The Civil Rights Movement
had not yet reached our very white school
and Vietnam was a year away.

Prom night was our Mardi Gras,
our Times Square on New Year's Eve,
and we lapped up the moments
as if there were no tomorrow.
We flirted, teased and postured in order
to look the way we thought was most attractive.
It mattered little that I couldn't dance that well
because I was dancing wonderfully
in my heart and mind
and that was all that mattered.
We wanted that night to last forever.

Fragments of Life

The priorities of reality and life were destined
to overshadow the light-hearted joy of that evening,
yet the celebration still lingers in the recesses
of my memory nearly fifty years later.
Yes, life would become much more serious for us.
But we had lived a night we would never forget.

Retrospectives

My Buddy Bobby

"Bang, bang, you're dead!"
I said to my best friend, Bobby,
as we played war most
every day a long time ago.
We both had machine guns
made of broomsticks and
we'd shoot at each other
for hours to win the war.

Bobby and I grew up
and carried real guns in '65
when we were teenagers.
Before that we didn't know
war was so very "real".

Bobby and I went off to do
our duty in an awful war.
We both came back in '66.
I walked off the plane
with a limp while he was
carried off in a casket.
Bang, bang, he was dead.

No more war for me and
no broomsticks made into
machine guns for my kids.
I remember too well
what war and guns did
to my buddy, Bobby.

At 43

In the midst of it all,
at 43, at the peak
of my productivity,
of climbing my ladder,
I took off my watch,
threw it on the floor
and laughed,
laughed out loud,
uncontrollably,
rolling on the floor
with the children
who were more
alive than I.

A time outside of time,
not noted on my
expensive watch.
A time treasured,
a time made eternal,
a time to be remembered
by kids, by a dad.

Retrospectives

One Look Back

So, without being aware,
we lived, we laughed,
loved, cried, dreamed
and spent our days.
But did we really know
what we were doing,
what we were feeling
while we laughed,
loved, cried, dreamed
and lived our days?

On this last day I look
back to the times we had,
the times of our lives.
Our time, a time that
replays only in the minds
of the two of us,
and soon, only you.

Fragments of Life

1955

Hot, hot in the middle of a summer day
in central Arkansas,
one fan in the entire house.
It's Sunday, just home from church,
sweating beneath the starched shirt
and scratchy gray slacks,
both feeling two sizes too big.
I get a washcloth to dry the hair oil
that's trickling down my forehead.

Dad enters the house.
His loud voice and heavy walk
set the atmosphere for this Sabbath Day.
He stayed home from church, as usual,
to work in his truck garden.
He walks through the house
in his sweaty, dirty overalls
and plops down in front of the TV
with tea in hand to watch baseball.

I'm bringing my religion home once again
to stand the test of Daddy's skepticism.

Retrospectives

We Were Dancing

Just yesterday we were dancing,
moving to the music.
We were dancing,
holding one another
as we swept across the floor,
going where we wanted,
one way and then another way.
The music played on.
But today the music is gone
and there is no dancing.

Therapeutic Eyes

Today I awoke to face the world
as if yesterday never existed,
as if its odors and its stains
had been washed away.
I began my day with the belief
that "I" was in charge.
Hardly two hours passed before
I was struck by the realization
that my life was not actually
starting afresh this new day.
Yesterdays reared their heads.
The past swept over me as if
I were standing under a waterfall.

Yesterdays accumulate
and wind their way
through all our new days,
creating stains that cannot
be eradicated by will power
or by good intentions.
Long ago, obscure yesterdays
continue to guide our thinking,
sway our judgment,
stimulate our fixations.

Retrospectives

God help me face the future
with hope and fortitude.
Lead me to acknowledge
the scars, the terrors, the miseries
of yesterdays I have wanted to forget.
Help me unload the baggage
that can so easily slow my progress
through today and tomorrow.

Lord, give me therapeutic eyes
and courageous vision.

The Child You Are

Down the path of broken dreams,
across the fields of images past,
forgotten thoughts of tense nights
filled with anxiety and fearful dread,
emotions lie in tender sleep
waiting for the searching heart.

Awake, sleeping memory.
Hear once more the sounds of
the dangerous days of your childhood
to help you recognize and understand
the source of your compulsions,
the seeds of your addictions.

Awake the child of dread
whose playfulness was stunted
by flight from the terrible reality.
Bring back that child.
Raise her yourself in a
gentler place of hope and cheer,
a home that nourishes
the child you were,
the child you are.

Retrospectives

Setting My Face

So much time has passed,
more than sixty years now,
more memories than I can recall,
more days than I ever imagined
when I was a young boy
of eight or nine
with so much of life ahead.
People in their sixties
seemed old, very old.
And here I am,
though I do not admit
to being old.

There's a lot to look back on.
Most of life has passed.
But with the remainder
I'll set my face firmly
to the wind and
to the unknown future.

Returning

There seemed to be
so much effort to living then.
Every day, every waking moment
held tasks to be done,
chores to finish.
Even on the holidays,
especially on the holidays,
preparations were necessary.
Relatives were coming to our home
or we were packing necessities
to take to their homes.
Then the cleaning up
and making ready to return
to our ordinary routines.

How I longed, dreamed
of the chance to leave
that discipline of existence,
to get away from the drudgery
that was required,
to find the freedom
that called to me
from within and without.

Retrospectives

Now, after years of being away
from the tasks of the home place,
I'm longing to return,
to recover the predictable,
to resume the daily duties,
to find freedom at home again.

Remembering

Ticking clock moves forward,
never backward.
Calendar speaks of tomorrows
and is trashed when tomorrows
become yesterdays.

Children await adulthood,
parents await an empty nest,
older adults await retirement.
No one takes time to look back,
no one remembers.

Black athlete goes high in the draft,
not thinking of an ancestor
who brought a high price on the block.

Jewish merchant's time is
consumed with business plans,
no time for reflection
on Dauchau, Treblinka
and other places that reek
of the deaths of his ancestors.

Retrospectives

Women take for granted
their right to vote,
their right to seek elected office.
Do they think of their sisters
who opened those doors?

Christians await a Rapture,
neglecting the lessons of the Cross.

No one truly looks back,
no one truly remembers.

Blank Pages

Turning my mind back
to particular years of youth,
I discover some blank pages.
There is no memory,
and I wonder.

Was there nothing learned,
or was there no joy
to record on those pages?
Or were those days too painful
to bring to remembrance?

There are too many leaves
of unrecalled experience
that have vanished from sight
and from my mind.

Retrospectives

No One Knows

No one knows
but the heart
what memories
lie deep within us,
stirring emotions,
thinking about how life was
and how it could have been.

Oh, what the days have brought
and what a journey
we have traveled.
Those who have gone on
and those who remain,
they are still alive
within our memory.

Little Boy

For all my years of life
and the evolution of "me"
through experience and education,
I am still the small boy of yesterday,
the one from 1951 or perhaps '52.
There are feelings and impulses
that seem to be immune
to education and experience.
These feelings and impulses
spring from the little me who has
never quite become fully grown.

There were fears I learned
back then, fears that have not
been completely driven away.
And so while I walk around as a
fully grown and well-furnished man,
there is a child tucked away
beneath the larger clothes
and the deeper voice.

In so many ways we will
always be what we were then:
little boys and little girls.
Unrecognizable as they now
are behind our façades,
they are with us still.

Images

Images of childhood
remain clear,
indelibly photographed
by my mind and heart.

A bag swing,
the black walnut tree
in the back with its
bright red leaves of fall,
the dirt road in front
of our small house.

Images, and feelings
remembered,
will always remain.

Fragments of Life

House at Mars Hill

Three-story house
with a wrap-around porch,
built on a grand lot
with a scenic view
of the town below and
the surrounding mountains.
It is an old, yet well-maintained
wooden house that borders
the old Baptist church and
the college founded in 1856.

Walking past the house
one observes a vast green field,
a plot that gradually tapers off
down a long, long slope
to a valley far below.

Retrospectives

Looking back at the huge
structure and its yards,
I envisioned the generations
of grandparents, parents
and children who have
called this place home,
the place that provided
to them the setting for
beginnings,
celebrations,
painful departures,
unbearable griefs
and joyous reunions.

To those who have
inhabited this house
the structure afforded
peaceful sanctuary for
their ever-changing lives.

Fragments of Life

Childishness

We had fun
in those former days
when we were too young
to worry about the world.
We threw water balloons
at one another
and we sang in chorus
like sweat bees
while walking the corridors
of our junior high school.
We were simple,
silly kids, rarely serious.
We hoisted outhouses into trees,
we swung from bag swings
high up in the old oak trees,
we skinny-dipped in the pond.

But then we got older
and became serious about life.
We learned not to joke
or to play pranks or to risk
swinging from trees.
Now, in the midst of my
pressure-filled days,
I often long to go back
and swing from a bag swing
in one of the old oak trees.

Aromas

The scents of tomato vines
after a day of picking,
dew on the grass on an
Arkansas summer morning,
the potpourri of powders,
perfumes and polish
on Mama's dresser,
Daddy's Old Spice cologne
and leather shoes,
my brother's new
Alvin Dark baseball glove,
cowboy boots and the
red liquid polish to shine them.

Aromas such as these
evoke memories of long ago
in the recesses of my mind.

⇀Lights for the Journey↽

I think I don't regret a single "excess" of my responsive youth — I only regret, in my chilled age, certain occasions and possibilities I didn't embrace.

— Henry James

The Difficult Days

So when the difficult days come,
reflect on those who preceded you,
those whose maturity and courage
were bought at inflated prices,
those who gave of their affection
in the midst of the struggle
with wars, droughts and the
lean days of the Depression,
those whose love remained steadfast
through sadness and sorrow,
through illness and death.

Reflect on those brave souls
and find renewed hope
for the struggle on the
difficult, yet transient days.

When the days of testing come,
reflect on your Creator,
your spiritual parent,
and know that you are never alone
to face the fears, the anxieties,
the tempests that will,
from time to time,
shake the stability of your spirit.

Fragments of Life

During your life's journey
remember the path of your forebears.
Reflecting on their path enables you
to find direction and courage.
During your life's journey
remember the one whose spirit
always abides with you
in the sunshine and in the shadows.

Lights for the Journey

Light Piercing the Darkness
CHRISTMAS EVE, 2009

What happened on that night
two thousand years ago,
and exactly how it happened,
remain an enigma to me.
Whatever did happen
continues to guide my spirit
toward peace, faith, hope and joy.

There is plenty of darkness today,
just as there was in days past.
Yet the light always manages to prevail
through the fearful or painful moments.
It is the light that guided our forebears
through their earthly sojourn.
And it is the light that guides you
and your families as you make your way
through a world that sometimes
seems to be shrouded in darkness.
Remember that a stream of light is only
made brighter by the surrounding darkness

Fragments of Life

May the message of Christmas,
that which lies beneath and transcends
all of the cultural trappings,
abide with you and yours today and always.
May the light of peace comfort your souls,
may the light of hope fortify your courage,
may the light of faith remind you
that you are never alone,
and may the light of joy ease your burdens
and brighten every day of your life.

Lights for the Journey

Shine On

There's a light that shines in every life,
a light to illuminate the path.
During times when we lose our way
we need that light to shine on, shine on
to drive away the shadows,
the darkness that envelops our lives.

Shine on, shine on, O light of mine,
cast your beams into the dark corners of my mind.
Remove the crippling fearful thoughts
and shine on to light my way.

There's a light that shines in every life,
a light to illuminate the path.
When the storms of pain and anguish come our way
we need that light to shine on, shine on
to drive away the shadows,
the darkness that envelops our lives.

Shine on, shine on, O light of mine,
cast your beams into the dark corners of my mind.
Remove the crippling fearful thoughts
and shine on to light my way.

Close to the Edge

Life is a precarious journey.
We live for a while,
not knowing how long.
We carefully travel our course
hoping to remain forever,
knowing it will never be
quite long enough.
We try to live right,
yet the dark often lures us.

We cling to a lighted path
that often grows very narrow.
Hands reach out to us
from the dark corners,
seeking to pull us in.
We strain to maintain
our lighted journey of life
as we walk close to
the edge of the light
and the edge of darkness.

Listen

Listen, listen,
if you can,
to the sounds that
cannot be heard,
the whispers and
groans of the soul
seeking to find the
light of recognition
in your hurried life.

Listen to the pain
that has been pushed
beneath the conscious,
that seeks an ear,
that begs for a tear
from your dry eyes.

Fragments of Life

> Retreat to the
> quiet chasm
> between the familiar
> and the strange,
> the known and
> the mysterious.
> Let the soul,
> the memory of
> who you were
> and the promise of
> who you are to be
> find a place of welcome
> within the space of
> your existence.

You Were There

You were there.
You never left me
when all the
others ran away.
You were there.
You gave me courage
when the night
ruled the day.

You were there.
You stood beside me
when all the others
would not stay.
You were there.
You gave meaning
in the night,
you were the day.

The Crossing

She crossed my path
unexpectedly, accidentally,
and smiled at me,
touching my hand.
Feelings that had lain
dormant for years
came to life once again.

Oh, how I wanted to stay
in the warmth of that smile,
that touch, that presence.
I wanted to stay and enjoy
the feelings of youth, of freedom.

But at that point in time
the smile and the touch
were only there for the journey,
to make it easier,
to make it lighter,
as my smile and my touch
were for her.

So while I could not stay
in the presence of that smile,
I could look over my shoulder
and know that her warmth
was never far away.

To Sleep

To sleep is to concede
that energy is limited.
It is to yield to fatigue,
to give up control.
Sleep is childlike;
we surrender to slumber
trusting that we will
awake to greet the sunrise.

Sleep is the medicine
that is readily available.
It is the home of
promising visions and
the renewal of dreams.

Let us sleep and dream
to bolster the strength
and vision we need
for the days of our lives.

The Road

And why do you sit
upon a soft chair
beside a road that
was forged and paved
by the sweat and blood
of mothers and fathers
from years past?

What right have you to
refrain from the task
of your own time?
What was given to you
was earned by others,
and what you give
to those who follow
must also be earned.

Lights for the Journey

This time, this era
is not the climax of all
preceding generations.
It is a time to create
for those who follow,
the next generation.
We have no right to enjoy
the fruits of those who were
faithful unto death if we
do not share their creed:
sacrifice and service.

Rise up from your chair
of ease and step onto
the road of history.
Get to the task at hand
and record your deeds,
your life, as examples
for those who follow.

Staying Aloft

Staying aloft
steadies the soul.
All of our activities,
all of our petty pursuits
ultimately end in futility.

But the soul that stays aloft,
that stays anchored to the
transcendent, the eternal,
will never die.

Spirits in the Land

The atmosphere is full
of memories, of stories.
And as we listen,
the subjects of our stories
live once again in the
spaces of our minds.

All of those bold people
of faith and fortitude—
those souls who bravely
bore the burdens of their
doubts, their fears and
the lot of all humanity—
were bound to the soil,
the soil that would
inevitably claim them
and return them to spirit
and to the dust from
which they were created.

Those bold spirits live on
within our souls this day.
Their lives inspire us;
their stories give meaning
to our short-lived days
as the current occupants
of this daunting land.

Fragments of Life

Remember

And now, as you enter this new life together,
I urge you to remember the love of those who
have nurtured your lives—mothers, fathers,
sisters, brothers, aunts, uncles, grandparents,
ministers, teachers and neighbors.

What those have given you will remain in your
possession despite the distance of miles or time.
Their best wishes, prayers and affection
will go with you along your journey.

Remember
that hope is stronger than despair,
that faith is greater than doubt,
that the future beckons you to believe
in your purpose, regardless of the pain of the past,
that there can be laughter in the midst of sorrows.

Remember:
do not embrace your troubles and adversity.
Troubles and adversity will come,
but do not befriend them and treat them as family.

Lights for the Journey

Remember:
do not feel threatened by desperation,
for times of desperation can often provide
the strength and courage that move you to growth.

Remember:
your greatest possessions are your
unique talents and the limited quantity of time
allotted to each of us who has been
pushed onto the stage of history.

Remember
that love is stronger than hate,
that understanding silence is far nobler
than harsh, unfeeling words of judgment.

Remember
that the One who gave you life is the One
who holds your life, always and forever.

Six Mile Run

Wasn't sure this morning
whether I was up to it.
I was going to go for five miles.
But after running two and a half miles,
something within me pushed me
to go on to the three mile mark.
As long as Stevie Wonder and Michael McDonald
kept singing their soulful, rhythmic music
through my iPod, I felt that I could make it
back home without slowing to a walk.

The thought kept coming to mind
that long distance running
is a paradigm of the journey of life.
Running is a metaphor for living our days,
whatever number might be remaining.

We are all running,
and we're running home.
Who knows what lap we are on
at any given time?
We may have many more laps to go.
Then again, we may have fewer.
Who knows?

Lights for the Journey

In whatever time I have left,
I will continue to heed the advice of
my high school track coach and "gut it".
For me it is not an option to sleep late
or to sit idly after awakening each morning.

When my final lap draws near,
I hope I will be breathing heavily
as a result of the energy
I'm expending on my way home.

Ring the Bells

Ring the bells,
raise your voice,
for our time here
is all too short.

Let your days be
days of song
so that even after
your passing
the music
will play on.

Lift up Your Eyes

O downcast spirit,
lift up your eyes.
Allow no regrets or
sorrows to linger in
the depths of the soul.
Lift your countenance
from the sinking
sands of despair
and sing a joyful song.
Let your heart grasp
the promising future
and dare to dream of
peaceful, blessed days
for a new age has begun.

Fragments of Life

Leaves for the Winter

Winter's here again with
its bitter, damp, gray days.
Gets difficult to keep light inside
when cold and gloom
blow in from the north.
Brooding, somber thoughts
find their strength in winter.
The thoughts and the weather
unite to dampen our
spirits and our outlook.

Keep the fallen leaves close by
for those drab, dismal days
when it seems too depressing
to feel anything at all.
Pick up a leaf
and remember that
hope and joy are only
hibernating for a time.
Pick up a leaf
and think of good things
like music, laughter, love,
friends and happy times.
Pick up a leaf
and remember spring
in winter.

Listening

Listening to my
wounded soul,
I found myself
once again—
the part of me that
yearned to cry,
the part of me that
will never die.

Listening to
the inner voice
that spoke of
fear and grief
but also spoke of
love and hope,
joy and peace.

Listening to
my soul
has been like
going home
again.

Friends of the Soul

All those hours, days,
months, years of wandering
among the shadows of a
half-lit room of comprehension,
wondering what life is about,
where it is going, whether
there is any meaning whatsoever.
Hour upon hour of experiences
woven through the chapters
of unplanned existence.

Life's pain and sorrows
etch the most indelible marks
on our memories and leave
us mired in anger and tears.

Yet it is those enemies of joy
that also provide the soil for
the strengthening of our souls
and increase our capacity for hope.

Lights for the Journey

Daily Dose

These nutrients for the soul
are as essential to you
as they were to those of the past:
hope, courage, thankfulness,
faith, laughter, love.

Hope will be your window to
the outside when all the doors
seem to be closed.
Courage will push you to follow
the exciting, yet sometimes
frightening, paths toward progress.

Thankfulness will be your acknowledgement
of all that has been provided to you.
Faith will be your sustenance
and a reminder that you are
never alone on life's journey.

Laughter will ease the strain
and bring perspective
to your trials and tribulations.
Love will be the reason for it all.

Fragments of Life

Bright Morn of Day

Come forth, bright morn of day.
Chase away dark clouds of dread.
Drive feelings of apprehension far, far away.

Come forth, O sun, and radiantly shine.
Bring peace to this anxious mind.
Bring light and life to the fearful night.

Bright sunshine of morn,
heal my broken and restless soul.
Let me see the promise of new life.

Come forth, bright morn of day.
Cleanse me from demons of darkness
that stalk my half-awakened thoughts.

Brave Ship

Brave Ship sets its sail,
freeing itself from the
confinement of the shore,
the shore where it was created.
Sunny skies cast their light
and approving smile.

Days pass and winds build
and roaring waves crash
against Brave Ship.

Oh, Brave Ship,
do not turn back
to the familiar shores.
Ride on, ride through,
ride on, ride through
the tempestuous waves.
You'll see freedom
when you at last arrive
at the shores where
you were meant to dock,
never again to be rocked by storms
and tossed by the seas.

Ride on, ride through,
ride on, ride through
the gray clouds and angry waves
to your ultimate destiny.

Fragments of Life

A Light down the Road

Life is like a long, long trip
over a winding road.
We walk in the direction of light,
gaining assurance
from the road signs along the way.

Traveling on, traveling on
without actually possessing anything,
while having more "possessions"
than are truly necessary.

We stumble and we sometimes fall,
yet the joys of the journey
provide strength and speed
as we travel ever so persistently
toward the light
at the end of our road.

Perspectives

Let us endeavor to live so that when we come to die even the undertaker will be sorry.

— Mark Twain

Maturity

We grow so fast,
losing our innocence,
developing calluses on
nerve endings to survive.

And when did we last cry?
Tears are muted behind
our mature masks that
age so ungracefully,
countenances crying silently.

Laughter is too often
a rare reaction for grown
sensible minds that repress
the humor of our comic selves.

But we humans, with all
our quirks and foibles,
are actually a very funny lot.
Too bad that maturity
is accompanied by a loss
of the spontaneity that
is characteristic of children,
who have not yet learned
to suppress their emotions.
Oh, what we lose when
we grow up too much!

Fragments of Life

Laughing

Laughing, dancing,
singing, playing
my way through life.
It's all supposed to
get more serious, or
so it seems—but why?

Why should the mug
in the mirror always
have a dour expression?
Why can't it be laughing
like children who know
that the cares of life have
no hold on their spirits.

Laugh with Me

Take a moment to laugh with me
in the midst of all that is serious.
There is more than enough
to be serious about—working,
earning a living, suffering,
paying taxes, raising children,
caring for the elderly, the dying.
And yet, humor and laughter
can be found in all of that.
There is and will never be
anything so serious that it is
beyond the reach of faith.
So I will laugh.
Laugh with me.

Gratitude

The years have aged us.
They have taught us
much and at such a cost.

Yet we are young in our hope
and youthful in our faith,
for those who have felt
the pain of life but have
nevertheless continued
to long for life are those
who drink the cups of
life and love to the fullest.

Perspectives

Awareness

Living is suffering
and living is loving.
It is mindfulness,
self-awareness.
It is knowing both
our goodness and our
lurking evil nature.

For to be born is
to be both a victim
of one's fate and
an active player
in one's future.
It is a depressing,
frightful, yet also
exciting and joyful
existence that has
been thrust upon us.

Dream Life

Dreaming may seem like a waste
since most of it occurs while we are
sleeping and accomplishing nothing.
Yet it might be that our sleeping
and dreaming are as important as
what we do when we're awake.

It is in sleep that our minds are
allowed to visit former times
to wrestle and perhaps resolve
feelings and experiences in a way
we cannot accomplish consciously.
Our daytime dreams keep us in balance
during those days when we are only
able to carry out the mundane tasks.

Perhaps our dreams are the centerpiece
of our soul, since both are intangible
and give credence to the belief that
we are much more than flesh.
Our dreams for our children are
forces that never die as they find
fulfillment in future generations.

Perspectives

So dream, dream now, today and every day.
This practice will broaden your horizons
and enrich your life because it is your spirit
that provides instruction on the mysterious
and unknown paths to your future.

And on your last day, may there be
a glimmer in your eyes and may you
rest easy knowing that you have lived on
the crest of your dreams, and the legacy
of your spirit will abide in your children.

Fragments of Life

Finding New Ground

When hurried and harried
by work that awaits me,
I find relief and sweet renewal
by allowing my thoughts
to carry me where they will,
perhaps to a place and time
that never were nor will ever be.

Standing on new ground,
even for a brief time,
provides restful perspective
and transcendence over
the mundane demands of life.

Dreaming

Dream dreams, yes,
but do not fulfill them
in mere fantasy.
Fulfill your dreams
through action.

Remind yourself daily
of the dreams you harbor,
then nurture those visions
through tireless toil.

A Thirsty Soul

Like a thirsty soul
wandering the desert sand,
so is a loveless life
seeking a tender hand,
hoping to find some sweet
peace of soul and mind
in knowing that someone,
a special someone,
really cares.

Like a pent-up stream
that longs to flow,
so is an unfulfilled love,
longing to be more
than just a dream,
longing for the
assurance that
there is someone,
a special someone,
who really cares.

Baggage

I arrive at this morning like a traveler
with my suitcases full of memories,
ready to greet the new day
and begin life all over again.

But life cannot truly begin anew,
for some of the suitcases spring open
and remind me of yesterdays –
my home and my former selves
with their attendant emotions.

Though other suitcases remain locked,
their contents intrigue me for they also
hold keys to who I am, to my beginnings
and the price paid for my evolution.
They are the ones that contain the more
enigmatic clues to the development
of my present behavior and temperament.

So while I attempt to begin life afresh,
I am aware that I carry all those former
images and experiences, the ones
I remember and, more importantly,
those I cannot readily call to remembrance.

Reunions

Our reunions are so intrinsically bound up with our separations. Just as joy is made richer by the taste of sorrow and hope is made richer by knowing despair and the power of the resurrection is magnified by the agony of the Cross, the happiness of our reunions is elevated after a season of separation.

My spirit, my eyes, my arms, all that I am, eagerly yearns for our long awaited reunion.

Perspectives

Working Woman

The waitress came to my table,
a weary smile on a face that
showed the lines of many years
of countless encounters with hardship.
She was a beautiful woman,
though not in an obvious way.
Hers was a beauty that was reflected by
the inherent grace of her smile
and the quiet confidence of her bearing.

She was serving me,
a man in the customary business suit.
My glass and cup were expeditiously
filled at frequent intervals.
As the recipient of the service
of that woman of natural dignity
who was probably ten years my senior,
I began to ponder the way
life works for men and women
and the fact that I should be serving her.

Fragments of Life

She had my ticket ready by the time
I placed my napkin on the table.
The tab for my breakfast was four dollars.
I calculated the tip for the simple breakfast
that was served with kindness and efficiency.
A fifteen-percent tip would be sixty cents.

Considering the financial concerns
of the woman who had to make her living
by waiting tables, I pulled out a dollar,
then a second and finally a third
and placed them under my plate as I departed,
all the while knowing she was still not
fairly compensated for her service,
either by me or by society.
I left with an uneasiness of spirit regarding
the way in which this script was long ago written.

Perspectives

Cleaning the Commode

How many of the world's
leaders, business tycoons,
sports heroes, authors,
pastors, singers, generals
clean their own commodes?

Profundity always strikes me
when I'm stooped over
brushing the water stains
from the inside of the bowl.
However, I don't have a pen
at hand and, unfortunately, the
only available paper is tissue.

During those moments while
breathing ammonia, I've been
known to depart in fantasy
to my singing debut at the Met
or my walk on the moon.
My departure from reality,
though, is abruptly halted by
the reflection of my face
in the bottom of the bowl.

Spoken Silence

There are words that are never uttered
because they cannot be spoken.
The feelings and emotions behind them
are beyond expression and can only
be understood as the voices of the soul,
as when a young mother holds her newborn
or when a man gazes at the bride he has wed;
the unheard cries of a parent
whose child leaves home bound for war;
the anguish of a bereaved widow
whose companion and friend
has been taken after a lifetime of love.

Perhaps it is also the silence of God.
Though we cannot hear his voice,
we experience our connection with him—
that impulse, that tug to keep living
and to keep hoping in the face of
the world's and our own cynicism.

Silent are the voices of those
who passed from us years ago,
yet their enduring and eternal
love continues to call out to us.

Silent though our own voices
will be after we breathe our last,
our voices and our devotion
will ever remain steadfast
in the hearts of those we loved.

Perspectives

Seeking the Supernatural

The ordinary daily tasks bind me
in ways that keep my eyes on the ground.
Mundane duties, necessary chores
all conspire to cloud my mind
that longs for a daily encounter,
a whisper of the eternal, the supernatural,
the quality that is transcendent above and beyond
this earthly existence that sees, speaks and hears
but does not experience the essence of the soul.

My search urges me to turn off the television,
to turn away from the computer and the phones
and attempt to connect with something beneath
and beyond the sounds of my culture.
Surely we are more than flesh and blood
with minds programmed by the demands of duty.

A part of me resists going to the quiet place of solitude,
for there I might discover loneliness and doubt.
Yet I might also catch a whisper of the
part of my existence that is linked with the eternal,
the feelings for which there are no explanations.

Fragments of Life

Will my life ever be ruled by the clock and
the calendar, the taskmasters of chronos time?
When can one find time to tap into the timeless?
How can one understand that we are more
than bodies and minds in servitude to the events
that occur between our waking and our sleeping?

Let us not be limited to discovering the
yearned-for connection just prior to our last breath.
Let us instead make the time now to seek the supernatural
so we can comprehend our most sacred journey.

Perspectives

Unknown Days

So much time
in our days
is lost, void
of meaning.
There are always
too many days
when we bring
little or nothing
that is valuable
to the experiences
of this fragment
we call life.

Too many events
are occurring,
too many duties
are expected of us,
so the uniqueness
of who we are,
our genius,
is neglected,
left untapped,
remaining as
merely potential.

Transcendency

The plane circled back,
making a sharp dip with its right wing.
As I looked over that wing,
I could see the little community
I had left many years before,
the place that had once been my whole world.

In those days I knew nothing else but McAlmont.
Only one accent was spoken there.
Most folks never left.
Those who did never moved far away.
McAlmont was the lower middle class
with a fence surrounding it.
It was not a fence that couldn't be scaled,
it was just that the little town could lull one to sleep.
It was home, and you felt you might
never want to leave, or maybe you never could.

But there I sat in that plane years later,
having been sprung out of McAlmont and
into the Army by the Draft Board,
then on to college and travel
and meeting new and different people.
Looking down on that world I once knew,
I was feeling grateful that I had been able
to leave and spread my wings.

To What

To dream,
to create,
to love,
to embrace.

To design the
uncharted future,
to reminisce,
to remember
a wondrous past.

To wash the dishes
or take out the trash.

The former first
and the latter last.

Theologizing

After a lifetime of reading scripture
and studying the sacred texts,
listening to countless sermons
and innumerable devotionals
and reading the thoughts and
views of hundreds of theologians
and authors of spiritual books,
it has become apparent to me
that all that is ultimately essential
are the basic instructions we offer
to five-year-olds and the words
with which we comfort and bless
those who are on their death beds.
All else is merely commentary.

Perspectives

Stillness

The eyes close,
the hands fold,
stilled for a time.
The mind relaxes.
At this moment
there is nothing
that can be done to
change the world.

Yet an inner change
often occurs in these
still, silent moments.
A part of the world
has indeed changed.

Songs Unsung

When there is no
means for expression,
the music in our hearts
and the melodies
we long to sing
leave us in a vacuum,
empty and unfulfilled.
We are as muted birds,
violins without strings
until we can find a way
to convey the words
and music of hearts.

So every day there are
songs we must sing,
if only to ourselves,
so our spirits will
not grow stale from
the act of mere living.

Perspectives

James Dean and Fairmount, Indiana

Today, all these years after his tragically brief life,
I came to this small rural Indiana town,
best known as the home town of James Dean.
It's a rather inauspicious setting for
a world-renowned film star and cult hero.
That short life, the persona that
has not aged with the passing of years.
And though his highly-acclaimed career and his life
ceased abruptly on September 30, 1955,
his fame seems to loom larger year by year.

I didn't know him, and yet my spirit
was touched today by the character of this town
that shaped the life of that young man whose image
was rapidly thrust upon an audience of worldwide scope.
Looking at this early world of his, his home,
the pond on which he ice skated, his high school,
I felt I'd been introduced to the man behind the legend.

Fragments of Life

As I drove by the neglected three-story
red brick structure of old Fairmount High,
I imagined what it must have been like sixty years before.
Peering into the paneless dark windows, I felt the energy
of the adolescent girls and boys living that intensely
present moment of their senior year of 1948-49.
The aura of that year indelibly remains,
for young Jimmy was shortly to become a star
and, in much too brief a time, a legend.

After his passing, Jimmy was brought home.
His burial plot in the small cemetery is unadorned
save for a simple headstone that reads:
James B. Dean
1931-1955

Standing at the burial site I pondered
the essence of the life that,
though it began nearly eighty years before,
will remain ever young.
James Dean's life illustrated both the brevity,
and the permanence, of our younger years.

Perspectives

Going the Distance

All through junior and senior high school
I'd been identified as a skinny runt.
Trying out for the football team in the ninth grade
confirmed that I was not only skinny, I was slow.
One day during the second week of practice
I was carrying the ball when Mighty Mike Daugherty
put a hit on me that brought down my pants
and sent my helmet rolling for twenty yards.
Too much fun for me.

At every assembly, the football squad sauntered in
like a bunch of John Waynes and took their places
under the admiring gaze of the student body.
They proudly sported letter jackets that meant
they were special guys, the stars of our school.
I had to face the fact that maybe I was a weanie
compared with those hulks.

Fragments of Life

That is, until the spring of '63 when I tried out
for the track team as a long distance runner.
In my tiny community of McAlmont, Arkansas,
eight miles from our Jacksonville school,
I had always been able to run for miles without tiring.
So on the track team I found my niche.
We were like Kenyans, lean and long-winded.

There were no big guys in the mile or half-mile events.
As I practiced each day for upcoming meets,
I would glance over at the football jocks on the bleachers
and think "I wonder how long those guys
could stay with me on this four-lap sprint."
At about that time I was finding my second wind.

Perhaps

Is the lack of human response
to act faithfully the reason
for our unanswered prayer?

Is our misery too often
the uncomfortable place
of our own making or the
only home we can imagine?

Are we too quick to notice
the negative while forgetting
the goodness that has been
bestowed upon us all our years?

Have we too often forgotten
that those who raised us gave
us their most prized possession,
their unconditional love?

In our moments of doubt
can we think what our parents
would whisper to get us up
and about our life's tasks?

Fragments of Life

Have we taken for granted
the breath of life that is
provided for such a brief time
and that exists for the enjoyment
of our short journey on this earth?

Perhaps we are so busy confronting
the day and the future that we
tend to forget all of the bridges
we have crossed to arrive at
this bright, new and joyful time.

Lessons from a Funeral Home

Like actors in a play,
we perform our roles until
our scripts are complete.
There is no rehearsal
before the stage manager
pushes us onto the stage
with no instructions,
and we do not choose
those with whom we
share performance space.

Our works of compassion,
our loving caresses
and kisses are eternal.
They are gifts for all time,
as they remain long
after we are laid down
for our final repose.

We must live lovingly so that
those tender expressions will
serve as sources of inspiration
for those who remain behind.
After all, this life is merely
the opportunity to enable
the lives of those who follow.
Thus, we are more alive
when we have passed.

Post Easter 2010

Past:
I can't prove it,
but I ascribe to the view
that God's grace
is greater than
my inclination to forget.

Present:
It is by grace that
I am here today,
and its presence
is a gift like the rising
and setting of the sun.

Future:
God was there,
has always been there
and will ever be there
in spite of my doubts and fears.

Pondering

Pondering
the great mountain
that stands before me
and the possibility of
fulfilling my potential,
giving thought to the
vast ocean that stands
between what I am
and what I could be
is all so overwhelming.

But then I remind myself
that it is the mountain within
that impedes my growth.
It is only the ocean of
self-imposed limitations
that prevents me from
accomplishing my goals.

Paradoxes

We desperately try to grasp
that which is already within reach.
We struggle to climb to the
top rung of a ladder, not realizing
that the first rung was the prize.

We must experience pain to begin
to know the depths of life's joys.
The grace of God comes most
poignantly in our days of emptiness.

We learn from our failures.
Through struggle we grow.
Our lives achieve full expression
only after we are laid to rest.

Perspectives

Opposites

Learning to be strong
and to be weak,
to be intense
and to be calm,
to be funny
and to be sober,
to be diligent
and to be spontaneous,
to be mature
and to be childlike,
to be careful
and to be carefree,
to be cautious
and to take risks.

The full life knows
the tension of opposites.

Memorials

A thought put into words
remains in the mind of another,
to be told to still another,
living in perpetuity or
inscribed on paper or stone.

Thoughts not spoken
vanish like vapor,
dissipating beneath
the details of living.

So today I will speak
and I will write
so my thoughts
will continue to live on.

Music from the Heart

Where and when
did you learn to sing,
and who were your teachers?
Did you come to music
as a luxury, or as a need?

When you sing, is it ever
from a broken heart
and a memory stained
by sorrow and hardship?
If that is not the case,
chances are your keys
will all be major and
the messages will be minor.

Fragments of Life

In the Midst

In the midst of
all the frenetic
movement of life
remember to laugh,
to love, to pray,
to gratefully receive
what life freely gives
rather than dwelling
only on what you earn.

Take time to observe
the children at play.
Learn from them how
to become a child again
so that life, and you,
will never grow old.

Perspectives

Facing the Mirror

Facing the mirror,
the face I see is familiar
and yet so unfamiliar.
The eyes bespeak of
a myriad of emotions,
from peaceful calm
to anger, depression
and fierce determination
to make good on whatever
number of days remain.

I know, and I don't know,
the image, the body of flesh
that has experienced a rather
narrow perspective of reality.

In this countenance I perceive
the genes of both Mom and Dad
and I wonder about how much
control I actually possess
regarding the direction of
my future, my destiny.

Easter Now and Forever

Today is Easter, 2010,
a continuation of Easters past.
Those who've gone before longed
for this future that we now possess
just as we long for the futures
that our children and grandchildren
will most certainly possess.

Today is the renewal of hope
for that which is yet to be,
that which has already begun
in our hearts and in
the hearts of our children.
Eternal life has already
begun its work in our souls.
We are on the journey to that place
where peace and joy are finally found
and where we claim our lasting home.

The journey is not always easy.
Sometimes it is wearisome and hard,
yet our eyes and our spirits
look beyond the challenges we face
to the home that calls us ever onward.

Perspectives

Birthday

It's on the days of our birth
that we ponder
the meaning of our lives,
remembering where we've been,
wondering where we're going.
Will we ever get to
the place where we want to be?
And how long will it take?
Is there enough time?

On this day of your birth
may you be reminded
of the strength of your legacy,
of those who've loved, nurtured
and guided you to believe
in yourself and in your future.

May the trials of the past
remind you of your courage
and the love of others
who have stood beside you
and believed in you
when going on seemed useless.

Fragments of Life

May you find strength and hope
for this new year of living.
May it be a year of risking,
dreaming, celebrating,
dancing, singing, playing,
loving.

Though pain, sadness and tears
may find their place in this year,
may they never, never
drown the music of your songs
or the joyful sounds of your laughter.

Special Days

We all understand
that the special days,
birthdays and anniversaries,
deserve acknowledgment.
But what about
the ordinary days?

Too often we go to bed
and greet the next day
reading our favorite novels,
forgetting to recognize
that the ones beside us
long to receive a touch,
a simple expression
that they are loved.

It is a ritual, yes,
but also a reminder
that we are connected
in the same way we are
with our children before
they close their eyes in sleep.

I have the power of blessing
by extending appreciation
every night, every morning,
to those with whom
I gratefully share my life.

A Book

A compilation
of single, thin pages,
each one a slice
of the whole.

A compilation of life,
of brief, fleeting days,
each one important,
each one a slice
of the whole.

Perspectives

WALKING FORT WORTH

Concrete and glass,
construction is always in progress
but nature is scarce
except for the skies
which are not easy to see
with bricks and mortar blocking my view.

While passing a darkened glass window
I glanced at my reflection
and the reflection studied me.
Here, this intangible image of my likeness
was for an instant a portrait,
becoming part of that hard, durable glass
which would outlive my transient and fleeting existence.
The reflection was not me
yet it gave evidence
of the nature and longevity of our spirits.
Long after our earthly departure
there remain those reflections
which give evidence of the spirit of who we were
and of who we are.

Vicissitudes

Only that day dawns to which we are awake.

— Henry David Thoreau

Scar Tissue

Every now and then
I think I'm really
playing it straight,
the way I should,
doing my job as
husband, father,
person of faith.

And then without warning
I encounter the shadowy
areas of my psyche.
At such discomforting
moments I recall that
there is no complete
healing of the old scars.

Sadness

Sadness builds a
fence around you.
It dims the light.

Sadness whispers
words of defeat,
stealing hope,
stifling courage,
binding the nerves.

Sadness creeps over
and around the soul,
darkening the path,
daunting the spirit.

Sadness is a subtle slayer.

Vicissitudes

Root of Fear

I'm no more than ten years of age,
trying to sleep on our back porch
under a pile of seven or eight blankets
to warm me from the 20-degree weather
and the wind that blows unhindered
through our screened windows.

And Daddy is in the next room having
the DTs brought about by all of the whiskey.
He's reliving his days during the war
and I'm hearing the yells and groans.
I can only imagine the devils he sees.

Sleeping is impossible since I worry
that he might rise from his bed and
attack me and my older brother Tom,
who lies beside me in our small bed.

Today, as an older man, I understand
the never-ending vigilance I experience.
The fears of childhood are not erased by age.

Alone

I desire it,
yet I abhor it,
this solitude,
this silence.

And so
I turn on
the TV
to keep me
company.

The privilege
of aloneness
has become
a prison of
isolation.

Angst

It came to me the other day
that my ailment,
my real addiction,
is Angst.
How long do I have?
Can I provide for my wife,
my children?

Anxiety is the sister of despair,
the brother of sorrow,
the sibling of rage.
It crawls around on us
like stinging ants.
It's the malady that
compels the drinker
to find rest and respite
in the power of the bottle.
And it's no wonder.

Fragments of Life

The one who was given life
is not the one who cast the dice
in the first place.
The dice were cast
by two people gambling,
by God.

We bet on life and on
overcoming the perils of living
until we are old enough
to bet on ourselves.
And it's all so risky,
this business of living.
It's not that living is bad.
It's just that the demon of
Angst must be faced
at our lying down in the night
and at the birth of each new day.

Vicissitudes

The Preacher

Fiery revival preacher,
eyes glazed with
fierce intensity,
preaching about Hell.
Preacher preached hard,
dripping with sweat,
pointed finger jabbing
violently at all of us.
Hard-nosed preaching
from the "Good Book"
delivered with patronizing,
sanctimonious attitude.
Preaching with emotion
that evoked emotion.

Many times the text
was difficult to detect,
but it didn't take long
for a youngster of ten
to get the message.
We were nothing but
worms deserving Hell.

The criteria for a preacher's success was the number of terrified boys and girls who walked the aisle, which consequently dictated the method and the message. Foundations of a pathological faith.

Vicissitudes

Up Against the Wall

With my face
up against the wall
I could not see a way.
I was pressed, pushed
against an immovable surface,
unable to escape.
The pain was so great
that I wanted to fall
to my knees and scream.
Yet I could not move.
The wall remained.

The pain was heightened
by the thought that
I had brought all of this to pass.
I had failed to see the signs—
"Watch out for the wall!"
It was like a consignment
to a living Hell.
There was no escape
and there was no one
able to save me.
Up against the wall.

Sadness and Joy

Sadness and joy—
both are my companions
since your departure
two months ago.

Sadness that our life together
as friends, as family
came to an end with your leaving.
We do not write our scripts.
We can only hope to
somehow modify, recreate
what comes to us.

The joy is in knowing
that in some small way
you and I and our two children
took the lot that was given to us
and shaped it a bit to our liking.

We did not waste the pain
nor squander the suffering.
Rather, we molded all that we endured
to create a joy behind the tears
and hope beyond our years.

Vicissitudes

The Drawer Called Suffering

Most of the time the drawer is closed,
yet now and then I slowly and cautiously
pull the knob of that repository of hurt,
that storehouse of pain.

What do I gain by these periodic
exercises of masochism?
Why must I relive, rethink those somber,
unhappy hours and days?

Revisiting the contents of that drawer
is vital for both the present and the future.
The drawer holds the trials from which
I made my hard-fought journey.
Those are the woes
that helped shape my life.
It is to all those adversities
that I owe my present place.

When God Must Die

The God in my head,
the one shaped by
sermons from childhood,
must sometimes die.

When the god I create
cannot sustain me
through distress,
disappointment,
grief, anxiety
or depression,
this god must die.

Whoever or whatever
God is, he/she is
beyond my thought,
beyond my constructs,
beyond my doctrines.

So in the difficult times
I try to remember that
my mental images
are never sufficient
to unlock the mystery of
God and of my existence.

Vicissitudes

Temptation

Beckoning,
the siren of sensual desire
doggedly waging a war
against his powers of self-restraint.
Pondering the pleasure of
a season of delight,
he thought of its brevity,
its mirage of denouement.

The urge beckoned on.
What was to finally block
full expression of sensual pleasure
was the thought of comparing
intercourse to death.
What would happen afterward?

Assembly Line

Knotty, rough-hewn hands
working the art
of the assembly line
in this dreary, cold factory.
No time to look around,
only time to whistle
and occasionally sing
and be thankful that
his soul can still
breathe in the music
while his hands express
the bondage of his flesh.

Vicissitudes

Screaming at God

So why am I screaming at God these days?
Perhaps it is because of the years
of remaining quiet and passive
while enduring the abuse
of being held captive by fear,
of not complaining to anyone or to God
about the extreme discomfort
of being held hostage
by the false image of God
that was imparted to me in childhood.

Sad Quarters

Cascading down through
their tumultuous times,
all those hours, all those days,
moments without light
when they befriended the darkness
within and without.
Pain was the norm.
Rage and resentment
were their sisters and brothers.
Their love was their hate
and hate was always close at hand.
Such an existence, such a habit,
an addiction to the underbelly of life.
They cherished their wounds
and cuddled their hurts
and swore always and forever
to get even.

Vicissitudes

Joy is foreign and smells foul
to those who have become
intimate with woe.
And so they must chase away
every taste of good
with the strong drink of heartache
to make the joys go away
and to keep their lives in balance.
Oh those self-imposed quarters
where nothing makes sense
unless nothing makes sense.

God help the children
who live in sad quarters.
For even when the innocents
temporarily depart,
the shadows of shame,
the melancholic songs of sorrow
are their constant companions.

Limitations

Man of thirty,
ravaged with disease,
unable to walk a block
or even to stand
without aid of a cane.
His power is in
his wheelchair,
confined, limited
due to factors
beyond his control.
No diet, training
or outlook will
increase his ability
to stand or walk—
ever.

Vicissitudes

At fifty, another man
takes stock of his life
and concedes that
more could have been
accomplished but for
the barriers, limitations,
afflictions, addictions
that are as crippling
as a physical illness.

There's too much force
in the genes and the
history of some folks
to make it probable
for them to do much more
than they are now doing.
All the while striving
and all the while coming
to terms with the hills
we cannot climb.
Limitations.

Fragments of Life

Impediments

They come from without and within,
hammering away at the mind,
creating voids of shame, guilt,
sadness, insecurity.
The arrows of the soul's early enemies
that inflicted these emotional cancers
are devastating in their effect
on the future of a life.

Neglect and abuse,
be it physical, emotional, or sexual,
leave lasting imprints on their victims
and the victims spend the remainder
of their lives trying to sort out
the ever-present damage.
What began as an attack from the outside
is maintained by the attack from within.

Wisdom acquired through the years
cannot often overcome
the impairment of the soul
acquired in youth.
It can only lessen the effects.

Vicissitudes

Facing the Shadows

Addictions, compulsions,
habits, proclivities,
tendencies, whatever they are,
seek to own me,
to thrive during
times of boredom.
Fear often pushes me
toward emptiness, insecurity,
and prompts me to shirk
the responsibility of
effectively using my creativity.

All the defense mechanisms
are so readily available,
so close and such fierce enemies.
They are always there to nurture
and feed the sickness within.

Courage, find yourself!
See the enemies for what they are
and keep them harnessed
so the light of creative fire
can burn brightly.

Disturbance

The ideal state is tranquility, peace. Yet we seek growth and very often find it through our distress and our search for resolution and answers.

Peace is desired, but not at the cost of growth, of our journey. Journey is synonymous with challenge. Challenge unlocks the door to our evolution.

Vicissitudes

Depression

So is it learned
or is it left over
from a past loss?
Is it the chemistry
of our brains,
this feeling that
pulls the drapes
to shut out
light and life
without warning,
this feeling that
camps on the spirit
and causes simple
tasks to become
unscalable peaks of
punishing drudgery?

What happened when
the air grew thin,
the light darkened
and joy became
ever so scarce?
And why does this
overcast mood
inhabit my soul like
an unwelcome guest?

Bondage

Vulnerable little minds
assaulted by hostile parents
become anxious for life.
Impress the very young
with fear, threats,
repeated condemnations,
and those children will be
controlled by phobias
for the remainder
of their existence.

The child who is subjected
to constant fear and threat
will be the victim of fear
forevermore.

Vicissitudes

Becoming Human

It has been scary,
threatening, humiliating
to concede to myself,
to my friends,
to those who have known
of my professional career
as a helper of others,
as a minister,
that I am capable of
making the kinds of
mistakes I've made in these
middle years of my life.

At a time when
achievement and mastery
should reach their zenith,
I am demonstrating weakness,
failure, poor judgment,
loss of nerve, insecurity,
anger at the world
and at God.

Fragments of Life

I can no longer pretend
that I have the answers.

I must grope, struggle
and grapple for the answers
to my own puzzle.
I have had to face the fact
that I am painfully
and wonderfully human.
And those who remain friends
through my wilderness
will be those who
love the person
behind the persona.

Vicissitudes

Battleground

Every day I go to war
with thoughts, urges,
habits, fears,
memories,
and my failures.

I cannot escape myself,
my vanity,
self-absorption
and the limitations
that keep me from
seeing who I really am
rather than the person
I believe myself to be.

Daily the battle is waged
to grow beyond
my small range of vision,
the myopia that is
my dwelling place.

At the Cross

He had all of the answers.
They had been given to him
through his seminary training.
All of his degrees and certifications
confirmed that his educational dues
had been paid and he was
fully equipped for the ministry.
He was there for others,
to offer hope to the hopeless,
encouragement to the despairing
and comfort to the bereaved.

But the Reverend had spent
the last several weeks agonizing
in his spirit under a cloud of depression.
It was as if all of the gloom felt
by all of the people he had ever helped
had been collected and mounted
on his own shoulders.
He had no answer for himself
and his prayers had become
mere groans and wheezes.
He could only say to God
what was on his mind:
"Why have you left me?"
The minister had found himself
where Jesus was—at the cross.

Vicissitudes

Adversity

The storms of life,
how quickly they can
de-stabilize our tranquility,
troubling our spirits
that yearn for the
still, calm breezes
of a life without trouble.

A life without trouble
is but a dream,
a dream often turned
into a nightmare by the
harsh winds of life.

It is the wind of adversity
that moves us to struggle,
yet it also moves us
to gratitude
for the fruits of life,
for the joys of life.

A Waste

Untapped thoughts
begging for expression—
a book, a symphony,
a scientific discovery—
all lying dormant
on damaged psyches.

Potential shredded
by the callous application
of ill-conceived guidance
from injured parents.

Inferiority, guilt,
anger, despair,
shame and depression
wrestle against
the latent thoughts
and turn them
into merely daydreams.

Vicissitudes

A Day Alone

Monologues,
one-sided conversations,
one-person dramatizations,
one-person audience—
me.

A day alone,
waiting to hear a call,
to receive a letter.
Too stubborn or proud
to call or to write.

A day alone.
Malnourished soul.
How it needs to connect
and drive the loneliness away.

⇁Posterity↽

Death twitches my ear. "Live," he says," I am coming."

— Virgil

Go Valiantly

Go valiantly
through life,
my children.
Let not the fears
of timid souls
daunt nor dim
your dreams.

Go bravely
into the future,
not allowing
the past to reign.

Pursue the good.
Spurn the evil.
Live and love as
your Creator intends.

Fragments of Life

Like Basketball
FOR JAKOB ON HIS 11TH BIRTHDAY

Life is kind of like playing basketball.
When you first begin playing, the goal
seems so very high and unreachable.
After a while, though, you grow, and
with practice you learn how to play the game.

At eleven years of age, you're off
to a great start in the game of life, Jakob.
I am very proud of you
and the way you play basketball,
but more importantly the way
you are growing in the game of life.
Goals that you will want to accomplish
may now seem so far, far away,
yet with practice and growth you can
always achieve the goals you set for your life.

In the meantime, may you enjoy
a very happy eleventh birthday
and many, many happy days ahead.

Love,
Poppy

Posterity

To Rebekah
ON THE OCCASION OF HER FIRST BIRTHDAY—12/15/79

You are a pink, budding flower,
you are the scent of powder and lotion,
a beautiful bundle of femininity.

A dimpled smile greets me each day,
a smile that radiates hope and joy,
an expression that renews my spirit.

A year has come and gone entirely too fast.
My wish is that I could have recorded each day
of the year past, though I know that feelings
cannot be captured for others to see or know.
They can only warm the heart of the beholder.

Rebekah, your birthday reminds me
that this is not only a special day for you,
it is also a special day for me.
You are a daily gift to me, your dad.

Miah

She is a free spirit,
dancing and singing
her way across the room,
and the music she hears
is her possession.

Grace and beauty
are synonymous
with her movement
as she choreographs
the rhythms she feels.
Music, dancing
and comedy are
the passions that
bring her spirit to life.

Posterity

Maya

At first glance, this
lovely child appears
to be somewhat solemn,
but beneath her countenance
lurks a jester whose humor
appears in disguise as
hysterical expressions
and actions that inspire
laughter and fun for all
those in her presence.

Maya is a paradox
of serious playfulness
and the beloved
sibling of Liana.

Liana

The glow of her
radiant smile brings
sunshine to the hearts
of all who meet this
little angel, and her
countenance conveys
that no one is a stranger.

Liana is a composite
of both of her parents,
along with a pinch of heaven.
The warmth of her eyes
bespeaks of someone
who is much older than
her chronological age.
Although she is only a
young child, she exudes a
remarkable maturity of spirit.

Posterity

My Son Ryan

Hours of shooting baskets,
throwing passes, playing catch.
Piggy-back rides and wrestling,
afternoons we spent running
up and down mountains.
Tuck-ins at bedtime
with prayers and stories.
Times when I beamed with pride
as he played his trumpet and violin.
Times spent talking on the phone
with my college student and soldier.

And now the times of seeing
him as a devoted husband
and a patient, loving father.

I sift through his old
photographs and I remember.
No hour was wasted.
No time was lost.
All of the times are now
more precious than ever.

Working Man

What are you doing? she asked.
I'm building a wall, he replied.
*I'm building a wall so my wife and
kids will remember me for something.*

Go home, she said. Go home
to your wife and your children.
Give them what they will not
see but will never forget.

Posterity

They are Quite Perfect as They Are

Bright futures most assuredly
await my grandchildren,
futures full of many and varied
opportunities and achievements.

While their futures await,
I affirm that it is who they are
now that is most important.
As their grandfather, I know
I may not be around when
they reach their mountaintops.
So who they are now is
what is important to me.
In my eyes, they are already
the best they could ever be.

Love,
Poppy

Listening to My Daughter Play the Piano

Here she is at age seventeen,
so near to her grand transition from high school
to the wider world that awaits her outside the home.
Listening to her play Moonlight Sonata,
hearing the melancholy of that music
and feeling my own as I view the photos
of her younger years, I am struck by the
reality that so many years have so quickly elapsed.

I wish I could capture this moment,
but I know it will vanish just as
the previous seventeen years have vanished.
I reflect on the days, months and years
that I carried her as a tiny, helpless child.
The years, all the years, all the times,
the joys, the hurts – and now
we have arrived at this moment so quickly
and so rapidly it will pass.
A camera cannot capture this moment
for there are feelings that cannot be seen,
there are emotions that the lens cannot convey.

It is melancholy that I feel,
yet it is joy as well because I know
the worth of this moment as it is being lived.
I am profoundly sad and abundantly grateful
that my daughter evokes such emotion,
for my sorrow at her impending departure
is the worthwhile price of the treasured gift of her life.

Posterity

Letting Go

My daughter's tiny hands clutched the arm
of her little chair as she pondered
the adventure of taking that first step.
Grinning with excitement and uncertainty,
she finally began the tentative steps
to reach my outstretched arms
and a whole new world was hers.
She had let go of the chair.

My son left for college a few years back.
For the longest time he held onto
the handle of the screen door,
but after what seemed like an eternity
he let go and began his exciting journey.

God calls us to let go of the chairs, the doors,
the false securities, the lame excuses
and embark on ever more challenging journeys.

If we are to grow, if we are to achieve,
we must let go.

Kidnapping

When the kids were in the crib
I longed for the diaper-changing
days to quickly be over.

When they entered kindergarten
I thought about high school graduation.

When they finished high school
I was anxious for them to
complete a college education.

After that I anticipated
the prospect of them getting on
with their lives as independent adults.

Now that they are out of the crib
and through school and on their way
I'm finding, every now and then,
that I want to steal them back
to the way they used to be.

Posterity

If I Never Saw Them Again

My children boarded a plane today
and as I drove away from the airport
I wondered if I have given them enough
to sustain them in the future.
Will the lessons I imparted to them
give them courage in danger?
Will my influence give them
strength for the long journey?

Was there enough laughter, joy,
enough good memories?
Were there values instilled
to offset their valueless culture?
Will they exhibit compassion for
people and for nature?

Seeing my children leave
was more like seeing myself leave.
I am leaving and they will be staying.

And so I left you, my children,
with a hurried kiss, a quick embrace
and a reminder of my love.
Will you remember?
Will you remember the words, the touch?
Go bravely, my children, and
may I also bravely go.

I Watched My Child Today

I'm now in my 41st year.
Today it occurred to me
that time is getting short
and there are important goals
that cannot be postponed
until some future day.
I must run a long distance.
I must write an article.
I must study Spanish.

While debating my options
I glanced out the window
and saw my 7-year-old daughter
performing with her hula hoop.
I walked to the window and
watched her for a long time.
Hearing my hearty applause,
she looked up and laughed.
That moment was enough
achievement for one day.

Heaven on Earth

Love withheld and abuses inflicted
on our children plant seeds of misery
for their futures and, very often,
for the futures of their children.

And so it goes,
the unresolved pain and anguish
of a parent's childhood
are relived and replicated through
thoughtless words and deeds
directed toward the children.

Our children do not know,
nor do they care what injuries
we parents sustained in our childhoods.
They only require the possibility
of a little heaven on earth,
that which was intended for them
by their Creator upon their births
and that which they will find
after passing from this life.

We dare not interrupt God's purpose
by harsh and thoughtless parenting.
May we parents find the grace
to heal our own wounds and brokenness
and thus provide a haven of love,
joy and peace to those little lives
whose care and nurture have been entrusted
to us for such a brief, brief time.

Fragments of Life

Grandfather, Father, Son

In the midst of a flap
between the two of us
my ten-year-old son
stormed out of the house,
slamming the door shut.
It never occurred to me
that he would do that,
just walk away while
I was yelling at him.

Boy, it's a good thing
he wasn't being raised
by his grandpa 'cause
he would have never
gotten away with that.

And as I stood there
I realized that my anger
had a lot to do with
the fact that I was never
able to do to my father
what my son did to me,
even though I wanted to.

So I picked another door
and stormed out through it,
leaving my dad's ghost
alone in the house.

Posterity

Daydream

My 18-year-old son and I were sitting
in the den watching a TV show
about a father and his young son
when my mind wandered back
to the time when my boy was only 6.

I daydreamed that I was getting
another chance to spend quality
time with the little fellow.
The reality of those former years
had been that there never seemed to be
quite enough time for us to spend together.

As I played baseball with my 6-year-old
I realized that a voice was breaking through
my dream, the voice of the mature son,
saying as he strode out of the house,
"It's okay if you want to just sit there,
but I'm going out to shoot some baskets."
I darted after him, leaving the TV running,
to grab my second chance.

Dear Children

How I wish I could keep you from
the thousand fearful, frustrating
and anxious moments ahead.
I do not, however, possess
the power to shield you
from all that fate may bring.
I only ask that you remember
your past, the instruction given to you
and the example lived before you.

I hope you will always look
forward to the possibilities
of the future that awaits you.
The future awaits as a gift,
just as the past has been a gift.
As you encounter the inevitable
discomforting events of life,
remember your past as a legacy,
your future as a promise.
And never allow a single fleeting,
frustrating moment to make you
forget that you are a purposeful pilgrim
on the road from past to promise.

Extravagant Gestures

We are always getting ready to live but never living.

— Ralph Waldo Emerson

Languishing Untouchables

There was a time,
at the beginning of their love affair
and the early years of marriage
when touching one another was exciting
and carried feelings of deep emotion
and sensuality.
Their relationship now has evolved into a casual friendship,
they are like acquaintances who rarely touch
except on a perfunctory level,
the good morning hug and the peck on the cheek,
expressions that in no way portend lovemaking.
That phase of their marriage has long since vanished.
Fidelity is there as it always was
but one wonders what each of them secretly yearns for
and desires in the way of romance.
Both of them appear to capture fleeting,
imaginary moments of romance.
He perhaps in seeing a beautiful woman
and she from reading her novels.
So they lie beside each other each evening
almost as siblings.

Fragments of Life

They seem bound to an unspoken vow
to never repeat the episodes of their uninhibited, fervent passion
for one another.
They are together yet profoundly lonely and desirous of the touch
of the early years.
They do not recognize that the only intimate touches
that either of them will receive are those
from the hands of the embalmer
who will assist in putting to rest
the burden of their humanity.

Extravagant Gestures

Tribute to Ruby
IN LOVING REMEMBRANCE OF RUBY MEARS

Even in her 88th year, with health and hearing
failing her, she was childlike and playful.
She could quickly recognize the humor in life
and her chuckle was infectious.

Her most valued possessions were not
material goods, for they brought her
little pleasure and comfort during her final days.
What she treasured most in later life,
as always, were her family and friends.

The appearance of a loved one or a
long-time friend brought a radiant smile
that erased years from her countenance.
Family and friends were the garden she
tended throughout her long and productive life.

The gift of her love to her children
will remain with them all their lives.
Her four granddaughters will carry her love
and legacy well into the next millennium.

Fragments of Life

Ruby was the epitome of beauty,
both inward and outward.
Hers was a beauty that exuded dignity,
nobility and character—beautiful
in appearance, beautiful in spirit.

Her body was laid to rest beside
the love of her life in the city she called home,
the place where she devoted her energy and service.
The importance of her presence among us is now
measured by the deep sense of loss at her absence.
A family, a community grieves her passing
and celebrates her life.

Summer Smile

The smile was there
many summers ago
when all the days were
filled with good times.
The smile was there
to warm the coldest winter
when the chill bit so deeply.

The smile is there and brighter now,
and winter's chill no longer dims.
The smile of many summers ago
lives again, lives again.

A Home Where Love Lives

A home where love abides
is a place where laughter is heard,
a place where burdens
are eased by sharing the load,
a house where there is freedom
and space for all of the occupants.
It is a house where expressions
of affection are a daily custom,
a place where anger cannot long dwell.

Home is the place of rest and renewal.
It is the place from which
our souls and hearts are never far.

A Portrait of Carol

There is within my mind
a many-faceted portrait of you,
a picture that evokes warmth
and tranquility within the
deepest recesses of my feelings.

The face, the person
I visualize in my mind's eye
is mere thought, intangible.
Yet that image evokes
hope, peace and love.

You are a dream come true,
you are beauty incarnate,
you are the love for which I have yearned.
You are God's gift in full measure,
you are my cause for thanksgiving.

How grateful I am that you
have graced my home, my life
and my heart with your
matchless, magnificent beauty.

Parting Embraces

And what becomes of all the embraces,
touches of the hand and kisses
given and received between loved ones,
husbands and wives, children, friends?
Are they lost because they are not
caught on film or documented?

No, the times we embrace those
we love are sealed forever in our hearts.
They are like fragrant breezes that
bring joy and lift our spirits for the
brief journey from cradle to grave.
They are the validation of our humanity.

What Love Is

Love is tough and also tender.
Love remembers and love forgets.
It affirms and confirms the other.
There is space and freedom in love
that encourages separate growth
and unity in affection.

Love is patient and enduring in hard times.
It is joyful and playful in good times.
It is hopeful and faithful at all times.

Love is secure, always
fostering security in the other.
Love does not wait
to be aroused to expression.
Love is a daily discipline.
It is the aura, the environment
in which our hearts abide.

Love is the place we call our physical,
emotional and spiritual home.

Touching

They were about 20,
no more than 21,
a young man and
a young woman
caressing, kissing
as they embraced
on the porch
of her apartment.

As I jogged by the
scene of affection,
I envied the spontaneity
of the young couple
and wondered how long
it would be before I
would no longer be able
to envy, to understand,
to remember the
tingle of touching.

Love Redefined

It has been a time of discovery
to live with you,
for in the time that we've
been together I have
come to know
the meaning of love
in surprising new ways.

I've come to know a person
as friend, love, confidante
in a manner that was
inconceivable to me
in my former life.

And I've learned to appreciate
the truth that no matter
what difficulties may arise,
having a companion like you
transcends any disappointment,
any fear, any hardship.

Love such as this cannot
be purchased at any price.
It's is life's most precious gift.

Joy This Christmas Time

Joy, joy this Christmas time.
Joy to children far and near,
giving your dreams a chance to thrive.
Dry your eyes, children of the King.
Christ is born for you this day.

Joy, joy this Christmas time.
Joy to moms and dads who hurry to and fro,
burdened by life's worries and strains.
Smile and laugh like children of the King.
Christ is born for you this day.

Joy, joy this Christmas time.
Joy to those in later years who
remember joys of bygone days.
Sing, sing in this grand new age
for you, too, are children of the King
and Christ is born for you this day.

Incarnation

Some say flesh and bone don't mean much,
that the spirit is what counts most.
Some in our culture even try to make
flesh and touching dirty, to make kisses
and embraces cheap and unworthy.
That's too bad.
It doesn't have to be the one or the other.

What good is a touch, a kiss, an embrace?
All of these give meaning to spirit,
substance to words, expression to feelings.

There is no virtue in withholding my flesh
from those dearest to me.
It is, in fact, a crime to keep to myself
what should also be theirs.

Flesh and touch don't mean much?
Ask a grieving spouse who touches the cold hand
of a mate who lies motionless in a casket.
Ask that spouse five years from now if
that old flesh, unsightly as it might
have been in life, doesn't mean much.

Jesus came in the flesh, walked among us.
People touched him, embraced him.
He touched people and they were healed.
Thomas touched Him and believed.

The flesh is temple of the spirit;
it is good.
It is the manifestation of who we are.
It should be home not only to us, but also
to those who ask from us to be
warmed by the hearth of our dwelling.

Extravagant Gestures

History Rewritten

So why am I compelled
to go an extra mile for
those who are not "my kind"?

Recognition of past malice,
slavery and the injustice
of "my kind" requires far more
than a slight gesture of kindness.

A wretched history requires
a radical reformation
of the present and the future.

Glory Days

Where once music played
it plays again.
Old sentimental tunes
of bygone times
and memories of
our parents' glory days
provide the soundtrack,
the backdrop for our lives.

Men and women dancing,
gliding across the floor,
gazing into each other's eyes.
Life stood still when
they held each other and
danced to the vibrant sounds
of the Glenn Miller Band.
Oh, what a band!
What a sound!
What a time!

Extravagant Gestures

We now commemorate
those grand moments
as we take in the sounds
and the rhythm, as we
imagine that youthful pair
so in love, so alive.
They live again,
they love again
through our memory,
through the music.

Fragile Flower

Flower in faraway
field, not seen
nor smelled,
nor touched,
does not exist.

We two beside
one another,
seeing,
hearing,
touching,
exist.

Your life real
from mine,
mine real
from yours.

Fragile flower of life,
fragile flower of life.

There is a Love

There is a love that is not
in any fashion tangible.
It does not speak nor
does it touch my body,
yet this love is as real
as the blue sky, the moon,
a tree-laden forest,
the music of a symphony,
the delicate petals of a flower.
This love is all of these
and much, much more.

It is the silent nudge
of the early morn
moving within my spirit
like refreshing waters
on the parched earth.

It is the cool spring
breeze, the feeling
one has while viewing
the desert sunset.

There is a love that gently
envelopes my being and
carries my thoughts to
regions far beyond the
ground on which I stand.

All That Lives

All that lives,
all that survives
is what we give.
Who we are,
not what we have,
is our gift and our
assurance of eternity.

Our private worlds
die with us at death,
yet what we shared
through our affection
continues to live on
in the lives of those
who come after us.

Let no good gesture
or word be left
undone or unspoken.
Do not leave them
for another day.
Those intangible gifts
should be shared
every day that we have
in this brief, brief
journey of life.

Extravagant Gestures

A River Called Grace

Grace is a river that
never ceases to flow
through our souls.

Those around us,
those with whom
we share space,
long to experience
the refreshing
and renewing flow
of these waters
through our devotion,
compassion, patience
and enduring love.

A Friend's Gift

For years we worked
side by side, sharing
bits of our stories
with each other,
divulging our hopes,
fears, fantasies,
dreams and joys,
revealing our
greatest passions
as well as our
strongest aversions.

The friend became
brother, confidant
and provider of
priceless counsel.

My friend and I
no longer live
in the same state
so we seldom
see each other
these days, yet his
significant place
in my life remains.

Coming Home

Dream as if you'll live forever, live as if you'll die today.

— James Dean

Daddy

Sometimes my Daddy was a fearsome man,
given to episodes of cursing and raving
that could last for what seemed like hours.
As a young child I truly believed that he held
the power of life and death over all of us kids.

Daddy was the Law.
His was the first and last word and you
dared not cross him, disobey him or tick him off.
The Lord help you if you did.
The threats and verbal onslaught alone
caused all of us untold fright.
The red face and the fiery, crazed eyes
were evidence of his dangerous rage.
His fury knew no bounds.

Daddy's been gone for a long time now
and, strangely enough, I miss him.
I miss him despite the seeds of fear
he sowed in his children's psyches.
I miss him because I knew where he stood.
I could see and hear him.

Fragments of Life

At times I think of Jesus and the words he spoke:
My God, my God, why have you forsaken me?
I think I know how Jesus must have felt.
To be honest, I have felt that way a lot.
My God, my God, why have you forsaken us?
I long to hear a word, to feel a touch, anything
to assure me that he's there and that he knows.

And it's then that I miss my Daddy.
Angry though he often was, I miss him.
He was there; he was present.
As unsaintly as my Daddy was at times,
at least he was there.

I miss my Daddy.

Coming Home

The Skinny Bunch

The Staggs boys were a bony lot
'cause we were always on the move.
We played baseball, football and basketball.
We climbed trees, wrestled and ran
across pastures and through the woods.
Calories didn't have a chance to hang on to our
bodies since we never slowed down.
And snack foods were tomatoes from our garden.

I feel sorry for so many of today's kids
who spend most of their free time
sitting indoors playing video games
and snacking on foods that pack on pounds.
They aren't aware of the fun they are missing,
to say nothing of the exercise that would
be of such great benefit to them.

I added some luggage during my 40s and 50s,
but now in my 60s I'm literally working
my butt off to get myself back to the little
piece of leather I was in my teens.
Those youthful days were the lean years
and how I have missed 'em.

Experiencing God

It's an early, early morning in McAlmont.
Mama and Daddy are getting ready
to face the icy chill outside to go to work.
I squirm under a layer of several blankets
to guard against the cold and the reality that
I will also have to face the chill in an hour or so.

My parents' marriage is even colder than
the early March weather of Arkansas.
Neither of them can give to the other
what they both desperately need.
They are two terribly needy souls
who have been repeatedly bruised by life.

The memories, the scars and the fears
get the best of both of them on most days.
All they can do is to try to face their demons,
go on making a living for their family
and manage to get through the days somehow.

Coming Home

At church they tell us that God is with us
but I cannot feel God's presence
on this uncomfortable Monday morning.
I can only feel the warmth of my blankets.
I strain to hear God's voice, but I can only hear
the voices of Mama and Daddy as they argue.
Daddy is cursing and yelling in threatening tones
that make sleeping impossible for me.

God is here—but where?
And can God give some comfort to
those two who have faced so many cold
early mornings as they attempt to eke out
a living that provides only a small return
in both money and dignity?

Legacy

There is a conviction within me
that at the completion of our lives,
what will be important is not
the amount of money or property
we leave to our children and grandchildren.
It will be the legacy that cannot be quantified,
a spiritual legacy, the kind that endures
from generation to generation.

And with that thought
I'm reminded of my dear mother
who, by the world's standards,
was a financial failure,
a person who never enjoyed
the privileges of power and success.
Yet that woman who worked
the last quarter of a century of her life
for no more than minimum wage
continues to profoundly shape my life.
Her soul is still alive within me.
Her influence lives on in the lives
of my children and their children.

The richness of one's soul
is the most valuable legacy.
Those who are the beneficiaries of
such a gift should gratefully pass it on
to the ones with whom they share their days.

Coming Home

My Eyes, Her Eyes

There are occasions when
I know I'm seeing life
through my mother's eyes.
What I see, she sees,
for her genes and her blood
are so much a part
of my chemistry.

I see with her eyes
because of all the hopes
she had for me as a child.
I see with her eyes
and feel her presence
at the most unexpected times
due to the limitless love
she poured into my life
before I became an adult.

What I now know is that
I've never been "on my own".
Mother has always been here
and she will always be here
in my soul, my thoughts.
And she will see all that I see,
for the eyes of my soul
are the eyes of my mother.

Fragments of Life

She Still Lives

I am a reminder to the world
that she lived.
I am a perpetuation of her love,
her strength, her values, her ideals.
She imparted all these to me in full.
I am the recipient of years
of careful guidance and nurture.

Are there other reminders
of her constant presence?
Just look at those whom she loved.
That twinkle in my sisters' eyes is hers.
The faithfulness of my brothers' love
is hers as well.
There are others whose lives
were touched by her caring hand,
who were never the same after knowing her.
We are all an extension of her life.

Coming Home

The Old Home Place

Tom and I drove down the dusty road
to our old home place.
As we approached the three acre tract,
I felt my insides tremble.
I felt as though I were thirteen again,
scurrying back to the house
with a nickel's worth of bubble gum
in my mouth
and a candy bar in each hand.

We both craned our necks forward
to see our place of origin.
What we saw was a disappointing sight.
It looked nothing like it did when we were kids.
Tom and I looked at each other,
both of us with tears in our eyes,
both saying, "That ain't the place, brother."
And it wasn't.
As we drove away, probably for the last time,
we knew that the real home place
had been preserved only in our minds.

Family Time

As adversity puts
its wretched hand
upon one of us,
we all, family,
come together
to bear our part
of the pain.

This untimely
illness calls us
to bring our love
and cast it over
the misery of
the one who
suffers most.

The sufferer
finds relief,
family bonds
are renewed,
hope is reborn.

Coming Home

Dad's Overalls

How did I know it would happen?
I simply opened the closet door
and there were his overalls.
They'd been hanging there
in that same place for a year.

Dad has been gone
for many years now.
So why such strong
feelings and memories
rushed over me,
I do not know.

They were not feelings
of sorrow or grief.
It was just a sweet
moment of remembrance.
I hope that I shall feel
that way again, soon.

Fragments of Life

At Mom's and Dad's Graves

I remembered for a moment
their quarrels, so real
at the time, years ago.
Now their voices are stilled.
What they were discussing
is now of no consequence.

Do I disagree with you,
or would I like to argue,
you ask?
No ... but I would like
very much to dance.
Shall we?

Prayers

We do not see things as they are. We see them as we are.

— Talmud

Christmas Prayer

We pray for a new Christmas
that will dispel all doubts
that the one who was born to us
is with us still.

We pray that this Christmas
will redeem Christmases past,
those lived under clouds of war
at Saigon, at Panmunjom, at Sicily,
at the Argonne and countless other
fields of strife where the
blood-stained soil still cries
out for "Peace on earth, peace on earth.
Let there be peace on earth."

We pray that this Christmas
will bring new hope to children who are
alone in the night, ragged and weary,
frightened, hungry and cold.
May we help them see the promise
of the star in the East and the child
in the stable, a little child like them.
May we help the infirmed around the world
have a Christmas touched by grace
with the gifts of courage and hope.

Fragments of Life

While we pray for a new Christmas
we also pray for an old one,
one as meaningful as the night when
the Christ child was born.
Visit us, Lord Jesus, and brighten the
shadowed corners of our hearts
this new, new Christmas.

Prayers

Prayer for Gran

Lie down, Gran, and close your eyes.
Let us, your children and grandchildren,
now carry the burdens you've carried for us.
Sleep tight, dear one, we bid you
as you have always bid us.
As you drift into sleep
remember our love is close to you
though we may be miles away.

Lie down, Gran, and rest well.
The hopes and dreams of peace
and happiness you've wished for us
are the same hopes and dreams
we have for you this night.

So lie down, Gran, in calm repose.
Rest comfortably this peaceful night.

Facing the New Year

Dear Creator,
at the dawn of this new year
we find ourselves looking back
and looking ahead.
As we reflect on the past years
we feel compelled to offer you our gratitude,
knowing that through all our experiences
we were never alone.
This knowledge enables us to face the future
with hope, with the awareness
that your presence, your love, your grace
will continue to sustain us
from our sunrises to our sunsets.

We acknowledge that we often anticipate
the future with uncertainty,
failing to remember that you provide
strength each day for that day alone.

We give thanks to you for bringing us
to this day and this moment
that is ours to enjoy with laughter,
music and expressions of love to those
with whom we share this sacred pilgrimage.

Prayers

When I Pray

When I pray, I hear my words
and become too conscious of what I'm saying.
When I pray, I remember my sins
and I wonder if God can hear past them.

When I pray, I am mystified by the silence
that is broken only by my speech
and I cannot understand why no voice
or sensation is there to reassure me that
I've been heard or that my prayer was worthwhile.

It can be so very, very arduous to pray.
Sometimes I find it terribly difficult to do
and yet I am afraid not to.

And Deliver Us from Evil

Keep us from making excuses
for our lack of effort,
excuses prompted by the fear
of success, of achievement.

Help us cast off
the blanket of anxiety
and face the uncertainty
of pursuing the unknown
frontier of potential.

Help us give up the old,
tired, lifeless ways
to begin a new journey,
to risk the unknown,
to learn a new trade,
a new art, to embrace
the fact that each day
affords us the opportunity
to become a new creation.

Prayer of Thanksgiving

Dear God,
for all that has been bequeathed to us
from parents, family and countless others
who have blessed us on life's journey,
we give thanks.

For all the adversities and trials,
those unwelcome episodes in our pilgrimage,
the hardships that have served
as a refiner's fire for our souls—
because your Grace never left us,
regardless of the gravity of our suffering,
we give thanks.

For those friends who love us for who we are
and what we are without regard to merit or achievement,
we give thanks.

For all the heroes and heroines we've known
who have lived lives of true integrity and courage
in spite of near insurmountable odds,
those long-distance runners of faith,
those who inspire us to live in like manner,
we give thanks.

For times like these when we take a moment
from all of our worldly concerns to give
expression to the hope and joy you provide
and to acknowledge your everlasting love,
we give thanks.

Prayer for Courage and Insight

Lord, release us from our self-imposed prisons
of limited vision, limited faith.
Open the doors of our tiny, damp cells
and flood our lives with your light and warmth.
Free us from the need to remain
in the narrow confines of our small
physical, emotional and spiritual spaces.

Give us the courage to leave the security of our
familiar habits, our petty concerns and anxieties
and to walk boldly into the frightening
and challenging corridors of the future.

Lord, we are so afraid of today and tomorrow.
It is much easier for us to rehearse the past
and thus repeat it in all its familiarity.

Unlock the shackles of our minds and hearts
and help us see the possibility of a life of challenge,
service, compassion, love and self-sacrifice.

Prayers

Help us, Lord, to not hold back because of uncertainty.
Liberate us, O God, to daily fight the urge to accept
our self-imposed sentence as life's victims.
Deliver us, O God, from the urge to create an image
of you and your will from the false, misguided views
that we harbor in our imperfect knowledge of you.

Speak to us, trouble us, save us from the slavish tendency
to remain in bondage to those fears that keep us from trusting you
and the purpose you have for all your daughters and sons.

Our prayer and our desire is to experience your life,
love and joy this day and every day of our lives.

Prayer

I fold my hands
on the pillow
to pray for
peace of mind
and fall asleep
before I can
utter a word,
my prayer
having been
answered.

Time and Age

I have spent my days stringing and unstringing my instrument, while the song I came to sing remains unsung.

— Tagore

Trip to the Attic

In the dim light of a warm attic,
inching carefully across the rafters
to the containers that hold
decades of memories,
I walk back to the past.

With the opening of each box
of toys, clothes and letters,
I am reminded that
the past is always with us.

These items are mementos
of a long, often arduous
yet joyful journey.
Now tucked out of sight,
the keepsakes evoke a flood
of sentimental feelings
and remind me that
the blessings of the present
are gifts from the past.

Time for Laughter
IN MEMORY OF MURRY SOUTH

He knew despair and discouragement.
There were dark, dismal days
when dust smothered his crops,
when there was no work and little food.
There were many times when his
bank balance could not cover his bills.
Yet there was always time for laughter.

He was in the war, the Great War,
when the hope of peace was dim.
Yet there was still time for laughter.

There were years of hard, hard work
from candle to cane, 10 to 12 hours
6 to 7 days a week, when the calluses
on his hands became as hard as stones.
There seemed precious little time for family.
The harvest was weak, the labor was short
and the prices dropped to the bottom.
Yet there was always time for laughter.

Time and Age

There was the Depression that brought on
the frightening pressure of taking care
of his family, raising the kids, followed by
the mixed sorrow and joy of seeing them go.
The days of old age and ever-increasing
infirmity were often lonely days
of just reflecting and remembering.
Yet there was still time for laughter.

He knew time was running out.
His aging body was growing weak.
It was not a fearful thought, though.
It was a passage, like the dust storms,
the Great War, the Depression
and the life filled with anxious days.
He never lost his sense of humor.
He knew he would pass through
that hour and beyond it there would be
ever so much time for laughter.

Reunion

We will all arrive there someday.
We are ever moving closer
to that gathering of precious souls
whose lives left an indelible mark
upon our own lives and souls.
Our minds can no more imagine
the life to come than we could
imagine being born into this world.
Just as there was no intention
or effort on our part to be born,
we shall emerge in a new fashion
through no effort of our own.

We are much more than flesh and bone,
for these are merely the manifestations
of something far, far greater than
what is now visible to the human eye.
We are also spirit, just as those
whose bodies we laid to rest are spirit.
We will, we must all meet again
for that longed-for reunion
in another realm, another time.

Time and Age

A Time for Mourning

A loved one lies in state
while family and friends mourn
the loss of an irreplaceable life.
Grief gives way to tears
and comforting embraces.
Few words are spoken.

In the midst of the absence
and the vast emptiness,
the assuasive power of love
affords a measure of comfort.
Survivors are reminded of the
finitude of life and the importance
of not squandering one's days.

As the mourners depart from
the presence of one they will
memorialize the rest of their lives,
there is gratitude within each heart
for another day to live and to love.

Cemetery Silence

I find it difficult to walk
through a cemetery,
a quiet, quiet cemetery
of silent souls who once
dreamed as I do now,
the still, still bodies of
those who once knew the
joys of life as I do now.

Thinking about their lives
is like leafing through
a yellowed photo album.
Everything that was so real,
so tangible when they lived
is now only a memory.
Gone with them are all of
their yesterdays, todays and
tomorrows, all that comprised
their transitory, fleeting lives.

There are trying days when
I would prefer to turn the page
and just go to the next day.
Yet when I ponder the silence
of the cemetery, I hold on to
the present moment and wish
for time to stand perfectly still.

Time and Age

Anna

Anna sits drooped in her wheelchair,
not having the ability to raise her head.
To those who see her sitting in the hallway
she is just another very old woman
who is awaiting her impending death.

The room where Anna resides
is a virtual museum with numerous
photographs marking her life's journey.
A particularly poignant one was
taken in the summer of 1942.
In that wedding photo she stands
alongside her stunningly handsome groom
proudly dressed in his army uniform.
It was to be the last picture taken
of this hopeful couple since Frank
returned home from war in a casket,
one of the casualties of a war that
stole the hopes and futures of
so many soldiers and their loved ones.

Fragments of Life

I asked Anna about the wedding picture.
After a long silence, I saw a soft
smile and a glimmer in her eyes.
With great effort she whispered
"That was the time of my life."

There are also photographs of her son,
who was born in '43, and Anna's
grandchildren and great grandchildren.
I observed that all of the descendants
favored both Anna and her husband.

The beauty she possessed in that
wedding photo has passed with the years,
but Anna's former radiance returned
when the subject of family was addressed.
I was struck by the deeper beauty of
that spirit who had experienced the
tragic loss of the love of her life at
such a young age, yet had persevered
to raise her family with courage and grace.

Time and Age

Patriarch

IN MEMORY OF JOSEPH H. CASON

On a sunny fall afternoon
he was laid to rest in a plot
beside his life's partner,
not far from the lands he
had roamed as a young man.

Just two months earlier he
had celebrated his 90 years
with family and friends,
and on the day of committing
his body to mother earth
all who remained celebrated
the life of this one who
so profoundly touched us all.

Though he is no longer present,
he is somehow even more present
in those of us who knew him,
a humble paragon of integrity,
a man who valued family
above fame, fortune or power.
His stature was not attained
by any of his achievements.
It was simply the man he was
that made him the patriarch.

He taught us that true strength
lies in the exercise of patience
and that strength is best applied
through service and sacrifice.

The world was made poorer
by the passing of the patriarch,
yet the many lives he touched
have been forever enriched
by having known him.

Time and Age

Embodied Soul

At 80 he still walks erect,
kicking out his feet with each step.
Most of those he encounters are much younger.
Seeing his reflection on the window of a passing car,
he feels as though he is observing a stranger.
In his mind he is no older than 21,
though the knees and hips often say otherwise.
At the twinge of discomfort he pushes himself
to regain the gait of his former years.

A compensatory comfort comes to his mind,
one that softens the reality of his age.
He knows that he embodies a soul
that has been tested and tried in innumerable ways.
Life has given him more than a fair share of vicissitudes
and yet, in spite of them, he strides with determination
and the knowledge that this mere walk
is a testimony to his stamina, faith and courage.
Walking becomes a metaphor for his life.

Ordinary Days

There are no ordinary days
and no ordinary moments,
for this life is so very brief.

As the years pass
we hold our moments close,
releasing them slowly
and very reluctantly.
We are more cognizant
of making the most
of our hours and our days.

As the calendar pages turn,
we make more time
for communication
by word and by touch.

There are no ordinary days,
no ordinary hours
in this brief, brief stay.

Time and Age

The Far Side of Eternity

Somewhere, in another time,
perhaps in a distant future,
there await answers for all of
the riddles that life gives us.
And in that long-awaited world
we will surely be given reasons
for that which cannot be explained
on this side of eternity.

As long as we live on this side,
the burdens of the past and present
continue to weigh heavily
and often seem barely endurable.
We hold within our hearts
the spark of hope that the other side
will provide meaning for
all that has transpired before.

Without You, Without Me

Looking at the sky above my head,
gazing at the trees with their golden leaves,
viewing the mountains, tall and oh so grand,
I think about you and I think about me.

The moon gives the night a lovely glow,
the water in the lake flows gently and freely,
the cool spring breeze blows lightly.
But they wouldn't mean much
without you and without me.

I hate to think about the passing of time,
knowing that the sky, trees and mountains
will live on and on for centuries to come
but without you and without me.

Oh, the beauty of nature
will not be the same
without you, without me.

Time and Age

Unplanned Journey

For all the plans, so much is surprise.
We plan ahead with calendars,
agendas and appointment book entries.
Our journals, though, tell another story:
the ringing of the phone,
the arrival of unexpected mail,
a memory surging to awareness,
a change in weather,
the ebb and flow of moods.

So much is surprise, unplanned
like our beginnings, entering life.
No force of will brought us here.

Plans, hopes, dreams,
our efforts to wrest control
of all the forces, the intersections,
the encounters of fate,
are of no avail in the end
when the unplanned appears
and compels us to release
our tenuous grasp on life.

Time's Worth

And Time was given to me like a treasure, wrapped in thousands of tiny, individual packages.

Only when their number dwindled did I realize their true worth. Time had been generously given to me, and I regret that I did not give of myself more fully in return.

Time and Age

Tick-Tock

As time ticks away
it gives us fleeting moments
to touch, to embrace,
to gaze into each other's eyes.

As time moves along
from one year to the next
it appears to hasten its pace.
We try to deepen our experiences
by remembering the touching,
the loving, the gazing of former days,
hoping to add still better moments
in the time yet to come.

The hours quicken
and we desperately attempt
to catch and hold each moment,
but the moments slip so easily
and so quickly from our grasp.
The clock ticks away as we sit helplessly
in the rocker by the window
and observe a young couple in love
who believe their time will never end.
Tick-tock, tick-tock.

Silent Sounds, Invisible Images

The sounds of laughter, of joy,
of weeping, of pain,
the sounds of routine chatter,
of hellos and goodbyes,
the first greetings
and the last farewells,
the sounds of whispered affection
before retiring for the night.
They all had their places
within these rooms,
within this structure that could not
forever retain those sounds
yet now serves as a memorial to them.

The images of events lived here also remain
for each succeeding guest to visualize:
Hands joined in family prayer
over freshly prepared meals;
parents embracing children
at bedtime, at breakfast;
children departing for college
or marriage and a new home
somewhere far away.

Time and Age

Although other inhabitants
now occupy the house of memories
and know it as their home,
sounds and images of the past
will ever reside with them
as their silent, invisible companions.

The Young and the Old

The young in me says
"Get up, get moving,
jog, do your chores,
dance and dance fast,
meet lots of people today,
work late, eat what you want,
forget about counting
the fat and the calories,
think only of today and
don't worry about tomorrow."

The old in me says
"Stay put a while
and meditate on the day
before getting out of bed,
take a leisurely walk,
pausing to smell the roses,
slow dance, check in early,
cultivate the best friendships,
eat carefully and eat less,
think of today, yes,
but be mindful that
the tomorrows are fewer."

Time and Age

Sands of Time

Two lovers lay on the beach
under a beautiful moonlit sky,
caressing as though the night
and their ardor were immortal.

Night, stars, moon and beach
could not secure their passion.
It vanished like the sand
beneath their bodies.

Fragments of Life

Past Tense

There are times when I marvel
at how far I have come,
possessing four degrees
and the boon of substantial acclaim.

As I pat myself on the back
for everything that I have achieved,
I think of my parents,
of their provincialism,
their trifling high school diplomas.

Poor souls, my parents,
ignorant of psychology
and the effects of their upbringing.
My parents were so shortsighted
in their view of the world.

Yet I sometimes wonder
what my children will think of me
and my narrowness, my myopia.
That is how it seems to be.
Every generation considers
the previous one to be obsolete,
backward compared to their own.
Such smugness.

Time and Age

And so I consider the circumstances
my parents had to survive:
the Depression,
the terrible war of the 40s,
the uncertainty of their future.
Still, they raised and nurtured me
in the context of their
worry and economic insecurity.

I know that I am privileged
because of all they sacrificed
to afford me the advantage of education.
My independent thinking
is a result of their experience,
their hardship, their failures, their hopes
for me,
their tie to the future.

Middle Years

Some day in the future
life will cease to be
what it is today.
Like the seasons,
our lives change.

During the middle years
life teaches great lessons.
The value of those lessons
is to be measured
by their application
to our remaining days.

It is in the middle years
that we begin to accept
the fact that we will
not always be here.
That thought brings
beauty to the present.
Today is a priceless mural
for now and for later.

Looking back
and looking forward,
the middle years are here.

Time and Age

Frightening Freedom

At this age,
at this time of life
there are no more bosses,
no more time clocks,
no more deadlines.

All the freedom
I ever wanted
is now within my grasp.
Long-awaited freedom
that allows me
to sit in my rocker
or read for hours
or take a nap.

There is no rush,
no urgency,
no one looking
over my shoulder.

So much free time
is wonderful,
yet it is frightening.
The many things
I want to accomplish
make all this freedom
difficult to bear.

Fragments of Life

Before the Day is Done

Before this day slips by,
some thoughts
penned for the record:
it was a good day
with rest, exercise,
lots of chores.
Daydreaming,
though not much
about the past,
mostly in regard
to the future.
Thoughts of dreams
that have been deferred
and how these visions
might be fulfilled
before my day is done.

Time and Age

A Lesson Learned

It is this day, not tomorrow,
not next month or next year.
It is this day when we either
share our love or withhold it.

It is this day when we decide
whether we will allow
the tyranny of the urgent—
the never-ending tasks of
buying groceries,
getting the car tuned up,
washing clothes,
taking out the trash—
to consume our humanity,
our creativity,
our passion,
our very soul.

Fragments of Life

And so, it is my hope
that when I awake
I will not first think of
duties I must complete
but rather bask
in the glory of this day,
the love I can share,
and what my spirit,
my creativity,
can bring to this day
so I will not be merely
a slave to the mundane.

Time and Age

A Sign of Age

I saw it today—
a clear sign of aging.
The 18-year-old
that I still feel myself to be
saw a much older man
in the reflection
of my car window
as I leaned over
to open the door.
"Eek!" I thought.
"For such a kid,
you look really old!"

I made a face that took
two or three years off,
then grew impatient
and finally rolled down
the window to erase
the discouraging truth
of reality altogether.

The 18-year-old chuckled.
As he opened the car door
he was careful not to notice
the older man in the
rear view mirror who
was laughing with him.

Death

A vast body of water
stretches limitlessly
on the horizon.
The sun falls
beneath its crest.
A tide rolls and
sweeps away
a green branch
on the sand.
Now it is gone,
taken into the deep.
Will the branch
reappear on a
distant shore,
or will it ever
remain consigned
to the depths of
fathomless water?

CPSIA information can be obtained at www.ICGtesting.com
Printed in the USA
BVOW041409160413

318299BV00001B/3/P